STRENGTHENING YOUR FAMILY

A CATHOLIC APPROACH
TO HOLINESS AT HOME

Strengthening Your Family

A CATHOLIC APPROACH TO HOLINESS AT HOME

MARGE FENELON

Our Sunday Visitor Publishing Division
Our Sunday Visitor, Inc.
Huntington, Indiana 46750

Copyright © 2011 by Marge Fenelon
Published 2011

16 15 14 13 12 11   1 2 3 4 5 6 7 8 9

Our Sunday Visitor Publishing Division
Our Sunday Visitor, Inc.
200 Noll Plaza
Huntington, IN 46750

1-800-348-2440
bookpermissions@osv.com

ISBN: 978-1-59276-877-6 (Inventory No. T1136)
LCCN: 2011937803

Cover design by Lindsey Riesen
Cover art: Thinkstock
Interior design by M. Urgo

PRINTED IN THE UNITED STATES OF AMERICA

Dedication

To VLN,
in joy and gratitude for your inspiration

Special Thanks

— to Father Jonathan for your guidance
and encouragement

— to Joe, Jane Ann, and Lydia for your thoughtful input

— to Dad & Mom Fenelon and Dad & Mom Steinhage,
for your examples

— to the Fenelon Clan for your unwavering confidence
and support

— and to Mark. I certainly couldn't have done this
without you!

TABLE OF CONTENTS

FOREWORD

Having had the joy and privilege of often being a guest of Marge Fenelon and her family, enjoying hearty soups, homemade bread, and delightful company, I can attest that "the domestic church" is alive and well in the Fenelon household. During my visits, I sensed an atmosphere of Catholic faith in all its fullness.

I have long admired Marge as a gifted writer and storyteller. In addition to the energy, wit, practical wisdom, and warmth that emanates from these pages, it becomes clear that she has provided the fruit — the fine wine — of years of keen and perceptive observation of human nature, viewed through the lens of a solid faith in the supernatural mysteries of God — interwoven in the humdrum and day-to-day joys and sorrows of a wife and mother. Using the Holy Family's example as a constant reference point for her own blueprint for parenting, Marge gets it right as she relates how focusing on encouraging and expecting growth in virtue and character will lead to the only real, true, ultimate goal — holiness of life.

Marge has her priorities in order! Her guiding principle of fidelity to God, married love, and family, is *the* sign, *the* example, *the* anchor, and *the* testimony that offers hope to an often bewildered world.

What better tribute can be given to families in this year when we see our beloved John Paul the Great numbered among the Blesseds? We celebrate this year as well as the thirtieth anniversary of his own teaching and gift to families, *Familiaris Consortio,* where he famously states, "The future of humanity passes by way of the family" (n. 86).

May this book be for all who pick it up a source of spiritual strength, practical help, light, and grace. Thanks, Marge, for another savory delight!

✠ *Most Reverend Timothy M. Dolan*
Archbishop of New York
May 1, 2011
Feast of St. Joseph the Worker

INTRODUCTION

When I was little my father nicknamed me "Mox" after the old gangster term "moxie." If someone had moxie he or she had gumption and ambition. The gangsters with moxie were the ones who were always wanting to be in on the action, whether they knew what they were doing or not.

When we become parents, we're in on the action whether we know what we're doing or not. Our job starts from the moment of conception and continues into eternity. On the other hand, we have our own abilities, the Church, and God's grace through the Sacrament of Holy Matrimony to sustain and guide us. God gave us these beautiful children; he'll give us the wisdom and fortitude we need through his own inspirations, and through the inspirations of other people in our lives.

My husband, Mark, and I have gained a great deal of inspiration, wisdom, and fortitude through our involvement in the Schoenstatt Apostolic Movement, a Catholic movement of moral and spiritual renewal, particularly of the family.

It was founded in 1914 in Schoenstatt, Germany, by Father Joseph Kentenich (1885-1968), a German priest whose cause for beatification has been opened in Rome. Father Kentenich lived in Milwaukee, Wisconsin, for fourteen years, during which time he worked exclusively with families. It's from Father Kentenich's wealth of experience and wisdom that Mark and I have derived most of our principles of marriage and parenting, and from which we draw upon in our work assisting in the formation of young couples in the movement. The rest we've gained from the teachings of the Church, trusted advisers, and our gut instincts based on our own formation and Catholic upbringing.

That doesn't mean we've been perfect parents! Our kids will be the first to assure you of that. However, Mark and I have sought God's guidance and made the best decisions we could in each situation. When I die, the heavenly Father will ask me what I did with the wonderful children he gave to me, and I want to be able to tell him truthfully that I raised my children to the very best of my ability. Everything Mark and I have ever said or done — whether it was a success or a disaster — we said or did out of love for them. Father Kentenich taught "the family table is a table of sacrifice," and we've tried to live that to the greatest possible degree.

If everything you say and do as a spouse and parent is done with trust in God and love for your spouse and children, you will foster an attitude and atmosphere of holiness in your home, and your children will benefit. I pray that this book helps you as you work to strengthen your family, and through your family, the Church and world.

I find great consolation, direction, and inspiration in these words of St. Paul. Perhaps you will also: "Be watchful, stand firm in your faith, be courageous, be strong. Let all that you do be done in love" (1 Cor 16:13).

Marge Fenelon
Monday of Holy Week
April 18, 2011

Chapter One

WAFTING IN THE ATMOSPHERE

When we were trying to sell our last house — a basic, but sturdy Milwaukee bungalow — the real estate agent gave us some excellent advice. "Whenever you have a showing," he advised us, "throw a loaf of bread dough in the oven about an hour before the prospective buyers arrive and put a vase of fresh flowers in a conspicuous spot."

We did, the house sold after only two showings, and we made a small profit to boot. Why? Because of the atmosphere we'd created. Of course, we had no intention of serving the bread — and the prospective buyers had no expectations of eating it, either. It was the *smell* of baking bread wafting through the house (and boy, did we make it waft) that tantalized their senses. There's something about freshly baked bread that speaks of "home." The same is true for fresh flowers. Not only are they beautiful to look at, but also they give off a scent and impression that someone *cares.* The real estate agent knew that atmosphere sells.

Atmosphere "sells" to our families, too. When the scenes and scents speak of "home," our spouses and children feel they're welcome and in a place where they truly want to be. My mother-in-law, a talented baker and wise mother of twelve, told me once that she had some kind of fresh-baked treat waiting for the kids every day when they came home from school. It made the house smell wonderful and gave the kids something to which they could look forward. It made them *want* to come home, and it made them feel as though someone *cared.*

Mom loves to bake, but it took sacrifice to come up with something yummy each day in time to welcome the crowd. Even though she was a stay-at-home mom, the time and effort of caring for twelve children required more effort than a full-time job. Yet she knew what was most important: creating an atmosphere that would make her family feel at home.

It worked. Any of my siblings-in-law can tell about all the goodies in Mom's pantry, and how they couldn't wait to get home from school each day to have some. It worked so well, in fact, that when we were newly married, Mark frequently suggested that we go visit his mother. After a while, however, I noticed that Mark seemed to disappear shortly after our arrival. Initially, I didn't make much of it. Then I started paying attention and saw that he headed in the same direction each time — the kitchen!

One day, the curiosity became too much for me, and I followed him. I peeked around the corner of the kitchen door and found him standing at the counter scarfing down baked goods, all the while "Mmmm-ing" as he munched along.

At first, I was furious. I felt insulted and even a bit jealous. How come he didn't show the same reaction to the things I baked? I never saw him standing at my kitchen counter "Mmmm-ing" along! I went back to the living room, plopping myself down in the armchair for a good solemn pout. *How dare he!* I thought.

Once I got out of my huff, I realized two things. First, Mark had good reason to raid Mom's pantry. It was packed with delectable stuff, unlike the cabinets in our apartment, which were filled with staples and some items that barely classified as baked goods.

Second, this was about more than Mark needing a goodie fix. It was about his needing a home fix. Being there in his mom's kitchen, partaking of the same sumptuous treats he'd eaten as a child, made Mark feel at home again and brought back wonderful childhood memories. It was comfort food at its best. After that, I gave in. I realized Mom was a superb baker and had done an excellent job making that house a home, and I wasn't about to interfere with Mark's enjoyment of it.

Instead, I tried to incorporate as many of Mom's "tricks of the trade" as possible into my own homemaking. Since baking wasn't my forte, I did other things to form a welcoming atmosphere in our home. For example, I tried my best to be cheerful and to greet Mark with a smile and a hug when he came home from work. Sounds easy, but it's not. Often I wanted to just blast him with whining and complaining. Sadly, I admit that I failed at being cheerful more than I succeeded. But I tried, and I know he did, too, so that at least one of us was pleasant when we greeted each other. It's amazing how a smile and a hug can change the demeanor of the people and the atmosphere of the home for the better!

I also tried to offer him something when he came home: a cup of coffee or tea, a little back rub (*very* little — I'm a wife, not a masseuse), or even just a moment or two to put his feet up and relax on the couch undisturbed. Since I was still in school when we first married and worked outside of the home for a time afterward, whoever was home first became the welcoming committee. A little gesture of kindness would work miracles.

AN ATMOSPHERE OF JOY

"To maintain a joyful family requires much from both the parents and the children. Each member of the family has to become, in a special way, the servant of the others and share their burdens. Each one must show concern, not only for his or her own life, but also for the lives of the other members of the family: their needs, their hopes, their ideals. Decisions about the number of children and the sacrifices to be made for them must not be taken only with a view to adding to comfort and preserving a peaceful existence."

— *Blessed John Paul II, Apostolic Journey
to the United States of America,
Mass at Capitol Mall, Oct. 7, 1979*

Of course, things changed when the children came along. It wasn't as easy to smile and hug when I had a poopy diaper in one hand and a screaming child in the other. Nonetheless, I tried with all my might to offer some sign of welcome, even if it was merely a nod of the head and a weak smile. There were days when I'd had more than my fill of colicky infant and sleep deprivation. On those days, I'd greet Mark at the door and shove the screaming little bundle of joy into his arms with a few brief phrases: "Thank God you're home. Bad day. Take this ... child. Now. I'm going for a walk." Then I'd put on my jacket and take my aggravation out on the pavement. Even so, I tried with all my might not to take my frustrations out on Mark, and in that respect he received the cheeriest welcome I had to offer. Even under stressful conditions, we did our best to extend some kind of welcome, albeit a desperate one.

When the kids were in school, I tried hard to make their homecoming a mini-celebration, paying special attention to the first few minutes when they walked in the door. Whenever possible, I laid my work aside, offered them a snack, and helped them unpack their school bags. I tried to show genuine interest in their stories of the day and to sympathize or congratulate as the situation dictated. Sometimes they'd be absolutely exploding with news and at other times they weren't open to communicating at all. Either way, I always wrangled up some way to show my happiness at their arrival.

On the days when I had an appointment or other obligation that took me away during the after-school hours, I did my best to leave a loving note and a snack on the dining room table. It wasn't as good as a personal welcome, but at least it let them know I was thinking about them.

With the advent of cell phones, parents have the advantage of making voice contact with their kids after school. While it gives us in-the-moment communication, it doesn't substitute for personal, tangible contact.

When our oldest son, Matt, then a National Guardsman, was deployed — once for a year in Kuwait and once for a year in Iraq — we had the gift of frequent electronic communication with him. The Army did an excellent job of making sure the soldiers had access to the Internet so that they could e-mail and instant message with their families. We made sure we used those communication tools as often as possible. However, the Army had warned the families from the start that electronic communication could not substitute for tangible communication — letters and packages. They were right! There's something about holding a letter in your own hands that was written and handled by another person's own hands that makes the connection all the stronger and in some ways more real. A package filled with items that were carefully chosen and packed with love goes far beyond a sterile e-mail or instant message to warm the heart and speak of "home." Often we'd put together "theme packages." On Matt's birthday, we sent him "Birthday in a Box," filled with a complete birthday dinner (as close as we could come to it, considering we could only send boxed, canned, or vacuum-packed foods), streamers, balloons, confetti, candles, a card, a gag gift, and — of course — a sincere gift. It wasn't as good as his spending his birthday at home, but it was a little piece of home that helped to connect us across the distance.

That goes for our kids who live at home, too. Electronic communication conveys the message, but it's nowhere near as good as something that's been prepared by human hands, and it's definitely not as good as being face-to-face with someone who really cares about them.

Years ago, a friend of mine made a personal resolution to make eye contact with every member of his family each day when he arrived home from work. That may sound trite and inconsequential, but it's not! It's more difficult to put into practice than we may think. Parents can be pretty tired and even downright cranky when they get home from work, and they might not have the energy they'd like to have for their families. But paying attention is exactly what my friend did. It took effort to make eye contact with every member of his family and, as a result, the rewards were huge. The demeanor of his family and the atmosphere in his home changed immediately and significantly for the better.

Strength for Your Spirit

"Parents are the ones who must create a family atmosphere animated by love and respect for God and man, in which the well-rounded personal and social education of children is fostered. Hence the family is the first school of the social virtues that every society needs. It is particularly in the Christian family, enriched by the grace and office of the Sacrament of Matrimony, that children should be taught from their early years to have a knowledge of God according to the faith received in baptism, to worship him, and to love their neighbor. Here, too, they find their first experience of a wholesome human society and of the Church. Finally, it is through the family that they are gradually led to a companionship with their fellowmen and with the people of God. Let parents, then, recognize the inestimable importance a truly Christian family has for the life and progress of God's own people."

— Pope Paul VI, "Declaration on
Christian Education,"
Gravissimum Educationis, *October 28, 1965*

Strength for Your Family

1. What practical thing(s) can you do to make the atmosphere of your home more pleasant?
2. How can you greet one another at the end of the work or school day in a way that is uplifting?
3. What does contact among your family members look like? How can you add a more human, personal dimension?

Strength for Your Soul

Family Gathering Prayer

Lord, behold our family here assembled.
We thank you for this place in which we dwell,
for the love that unites us,
for the peace accorded to us this day,
for the hope with which we expect the morrow;
for the health, the work, the food, and the bright skies
that make our lives delightful;
for our friends in all parts of the earth.
Amen.

— Robert Louis Stevenson

Chapter Two

PRIME TIME

Supper time can be prime time to either foster or re-capture that atmosphere of home. Not all families can have supper together every night, but most families can eat together at least some nights. Regardless of how many of us were around, I always tried to make supper time festive. Notice I said "festive," not "fancy." Our meals were fairly basic: meat; rice, noodles, or potatoes; a vegetable; salad; and, once in a while, an interesting side dish. And, yes, there were plenty of times I served frozen pizza or canned soup!

My older kids swear I cook better stuff now that they've moved out. "Why didn't you cook like this while we were living at home?" they ask, smacking their lips and sighing in lament. Really, I hadn't noticed any difference in what I cooked, or how I cooked it, except, perhaps, for my newfound interest in Thai food, spawned when I got curious one day at the supermarket and wandered down the international-foods aisle. And I do remember to get the meat out to thaw in the morning, or even occasionally the night before, rather than ten minutes before supper has to be ready. Perhaps I do follow recipes a bit more closely rather than making substitutions and taking shortcuts. And I've even managed to (sometimes) get a rough idea of what I might want to cook ahead of time so that I can put the ingredients on the grocery list for the next week.

But what's really different? Let's see …. I haven't changed a diaper in a long time, and nobody really pulls at my sleeve anymore unless it's the dog and she wants to play. I have only one child to keep an eye on, and as a high-schooler he's around less and less. So now I can pay more attention to things like recipes and fancy dishes.

Of course, I don't consider that anything to brag about. I know some moms who do have a passel of kids at home and still manage to put wonderful, enticing meals on the table. And I know some who would love to drum up exciting cuisine, but health or handicap prevents them. And, there still are days when things have gotten so out of hand that I declare "Sandwich Night," and we get out the bread, meat, and cheese, and throw some veggies on top to make it healthier.

To be very honest, those "Sandwich Nights" make me miss the good old days when all the kids were at home and I was feeling frazzled and frenzied but oh-so in love with my family. It makes me realize that the fare itself was never the main attraction. Rather, it was the people and the place. We almost always sat around the table (as opposed to everyone off in the house somewhere doing his or her own thing), and we almost always fully set the table. Within reason, I tried to pay attention to the small details that added an extra touch.

For example, one little "trick" I stole from my mother-in-law was to have lit candles on the table each night. Of course, I have to admit that we did take a candle sabbatical for a while when the kids were at that pyromaniac stage of being uncontrollably attracted to flame and yet not mature enough to control their daring. But, I digress …

Candles or not, I tried to make supper time a special time with attention to how the table was set and the food presented. Few meals looked even close to the cover shot of *Better Homes and Gardens*, but I tried to pour every ounce of love and joy I could muster into the meal. That might seem like a lot of fuss to put into something that's going to be consumed in a matter of minutes, but this is about more than food platters and table settings; it's about forming an atmosphere that's pleasing to both the eye and the heart.

Eating together is one thing, but what about working together? Chore time can be a real challenge. Few children *like* to do chores, unless they're too young to do them, in which case we can't keep them away from the bottles of cleaners (which is itself a chore). Let's face it, there aren't even that many adults who like to do chores. Still, Mark and I insisted that our kids participate in the housekeeping tasks for two reasons. First, it gave them a sense of ownership and made them feel part of a greater whole. And second, it taught them important family living skills that they'd need later in life.

Some families we know divide chore time by room, with each child taking responsibility for cleaning up one room of the house on a designated "cleaning day." Other families "assign" a room to each child, partnering the little ones with older siblings, and requiring them to keep that room clean throughout the week. However, we seldom had time to do all of the cleaning on a single day. Instead, we worked on one room or type of chore each day. For example, on Mondays we cleaned the bathrooms. On Tuesdays, we folded laundry, and so on. Each day each child was responsible for a particular part of the overall task. One might wipe down the bathroom sinks. Another might clean the bathtub, and the last unlucky kid would scrub the toilet. I'd supervise, help the struggling, and do my own share. As they got older, they'd "graduate" to more complex tasks. Not only did this make chore time more manageable for them, but it gave the toilet scrubber hope that eventually he or she would be relieved of that duty.

We started our kids doing "real chores" at about the age of five by putting them in charge of their own bedrooms. They were required to keep their floors picked up and make their own beds. At that point, I outfitted the bed as simply as possible to make the task less complicated. I showed them how to do it and then let them manage on their own. The hardest part was keeping my mouth shut when things weren't perfect!

It'd be nice to say that every chore time went smoothly, and that we all worked together like little angels. Nope. We fought, sometimes scuffled, and often got grumpy, including me. In spite of the inevitable irritation and occasional conflict, Mark and I felt this was an invaluable way to teach the children how to accept responsibility, make a house a home, and cooperate even when they wanted desperately to bust the next guy's head.

Our goal, I explained to the kids, was to keep the house tidy (not pristine) enough to prevent the dust bunnies from turning into dust Godzillas, sanitary enough to be healthy, and ordered enough to be able to tell which room you're in. There's a trifold principle behind this. Maintaining a pleasant atmosphere in the home generates a certain level of self-respect — we are worthy of having a decent environment in which to live. It demonstrates respect for others — they are worthy of having a decent environment in which to live. It honors the Triune God through holy stewardship of the things he has given us, including our home.

We also tried to approach each day with an attitude of joyful playfulness — not easy for someone who is grouchy and incoherent without at least a half pot of coffee in the mornings! When we were home schooling, our days always began with morning prayer followed by chore time and schoolwork. The schedule continued with the Angelus, meal prayers, lunch, and a nap and/or some outdoor recreation, depending on the day's weather. Then it was on to finishing the school day, starting supper, meal prayers, chore time (yes, *again*), free time, reading aloud together, night prayer, maybe more reading aloud for the older ones, and finally my sitting on the floor next to one of their beds in the dark singing until they were mostly asleep (or at least until they faked it so well that I believed them).

I tried to make schooling fun whenever possible. For example, all our kids tying handkerchiefs around their heads, lying on newspaper mats underneath the dining room table, and painting Michelangelo-style "frescos" on large pieces of paper taped to the underside of the table. Some took to it better than others, but all have since let bygones be bygones. At least they appreciate the fact that I tried to add a little fun and interest to art class!

Even if you don't home-school, there are ways to inject playful joyfulness into your everyday routines. It just takes a little uninhibited imagination. Have you ever wondered what it would be like to do the dishes in costume while acting the part of an historical figure? Or, have you considered turning homework time into a Sherlock Holmes mystery?

Atmosphere includes much more than the physical appearance of the home; it also includes moods, attentiveness to one another (or lack thereof), feelings, and attitudes. It's not only what we do or don't do, but also the way we do or don't do it. It's whether we purposefully set the table or carelessly scatter the plates and utensils over the tabletop. It's whether we happily sit down on the sofa to enjoy a show together or plop ourselves down resentfully because they're watching something we're not interested in seeing. It's whether we say "excuse me" when bumping into someone or just push our way through. It's all the things both verbal and nonverbal that set the tone for our daily living.

We can take our cue from the Holy Family. They lived by five guiding principles: the spirit of prayer, work, sacrificial patience, pronounced obedience, and genuine, mutual love. How did those guiding principles affect the atmosphere of their home?

Our Lord spent thirty years living within the family context. His choice to spend the better part of his life at home with his family was intentional — a nonverbal statement on the importance of the family. Most of us know the Bible stories about the Holy Family, but we may not realize that they can tell us about the personality and character of each family member and his or her influence on the atmosphere of their home.

We know that St. Joseph was a carpenter — a tradesman who earned his livelihood with his own hands. We know that he wasn't rich — he and our Blessed Mother offered two turtle doves at Jesus' circumcision and Mary's purification because they couldn't afford a lamb (see Lk 2:24). And yet, Joseph was of royal lineage, a descendant of David, the greatest king of Israel. We also know that he was a caring and compassionate, a man of faith and obedience, referred to as a "just man." He could have publicly shamed Mary when he discovered she was pregnant with

someone else's child, but he chose to protect her safety and reputation and divorce her quietly (Mt 1:19-25).

Additionally, he followed God's will (spoken to him through the angel) without question. At the angel's word, he accepted Mary as his wife, fled to Egypt to escape a death threat against his son, waited there trustingly, and returned when Nazareth was again safe for his family (Mt 2:13-23). Certainly, he was a man of great love. When Jesus was lost, St. Joseph searched feverishly for three days until he and Mary discovered Our Lord in the Temple — a gesture that symbolized his selfless commitment to his family (Lk 2:48).

We know much about the Blessed Mother, of course, but certainly not as much as we'd like to know. Apocryphal writing (books that aren't Scripture but use the same style) — including especially the *Protoevangelium of James* — say that Mary was born in Jerusalem, the daughter of St. Joachim and St. Anne. While still a young girl she was presented in the Temple and took a vow of virginity. She took the vow freely, demonstrating her desire to give herself entirely to God. It's Scripture that tells us that when presented with some of the most outrageous circumstances a human being could possibly face, she gave her immediate consent (Lk 1:26-38; 2:9-19; 2:21-24; 2:51; Jn 2:1-11; 19:26-27).

Imagine being visited by an angel and told that you would conceive and bear the Son of God. Or imagine being warned by some old man at church that you must endure tremendous suffering, and that your son will be a sign of contradiction for ages to come. Then there's the water that turned into wine at Cana, the unspeakable horrors of the Crucifixion, and the inconceivable mystery of

the Resurrection. How did Mary handle these things? She said "yes" to God's will and pondered it in her heart.

On the other hand, Mary was also a woman of action. When she discovered that her cousin, Elizabeth — a woman of advanced age — was pregnant, she went without hesitation to assist her, crossing about seventy miles of tough terrain to get there. When the census was called, she was on the road again, this time alongside St. Joseph on the way to Bethlehem. At the wedding in Cana, she noticed the young wedding couple's wine had run out (a potential embarrassment), and she was on the move again, this time motivating Jesus to perform his first public miracle. All but one of Jesus' apostles abandoned him on the road to Calvary, but his mother did not. She walked with him and took his bloodied and battered body into her arms when it was done. Afterward, she joined the frightened disciples in the Upper Room, awaiting the Holy Spirit with them.

Jesus was the son of a carpenter and therefore also a tradesman. Fully divine and fully human, he was fully devoted to his family. Although he was the King of Kings, he never held his royalty over anyone's head, especially not those in his family (Jn 18:37). All biblical accounts show Jesus as treating his disciples with love and patience. If that's the way he treated his followers, with how much more love and patience would he have treated his own family? Scripture tells us that every knee shall bow to him, and every tongue shall give praise to God (Is 45:23). Just imagine *living* with Jesus!

As baptized Christians, we *do* live with him. We're members of the Body of Christ, and he dwells in our souls. And while we don't live with him bodily as the Blessed Mother and St. Joseph did, we live with him spiritually.

As Christians, we're called to imitate Christ, and Christian families are called to imitate the Holy Family in the way they lived and loved together. That begins with the home's atmosphere.

Based on what we know about the Holy Family, we can safely assume that they were a community of life and love. We can assume that St. Joseph crafted items for his own family with great love and care. We can imagine the Blessed Mother bustling about, tending to all the details both big and small, filling the needs of the family — and likely relatives, friends, and neighbors, too — turning

AN INTIMATE COMMUNITY OF LIFE AND LOVE

"Accordingly, the family must go back to the 'beginning' of God's creative act.... Since in God's plan it has been established as an 'intimate community of life and love,' the family has the mission to become more and more ... a community of life and love, in an effort that will find fulfillment, as will everything created and redeemed, in the kingdom of God.... We must say that the essence and role of the family are in the final analysis specified by love. Hence, the family has the mission to guard, reveal, and communicate love, and this is a living reflection of and a real sharing in God's love for humanity and the love of Christ the Lord for the Church his bride."

— *Blessed John Paul II*, Familiaris Consortio, *"On the Role of the Christian Family in the Modern World,"* 1981 whatever shelter they had into a real home. There is no doubt that Jesus participated in family life in a most animated way, and contributed to the household both practically and spiritually.

We can form our home into a "Little Nazareth" by striving to imitate the Holy Family. The Blessed Mother and St. Joseph were ever conscious of Jesus within their midst. So, too, we should be ever conscious of him within our own midst, and we should work hard to fashion the atmosphere of our homes accordingly. We should keep it in a condition that is worthy of his presence.

Does that mean we have to slave night and day to make our home into a palace? Of course not. That's not practical, and could even be detrimental to family life, considering the stress it could place upon family members. No, we're a family and live as a family. Sometimes things get out of hand because other priorities and unexpected situations arise that require our attention and energy. Overall, though, we want to be conscious of maintaining an atmosphere — to the best of our ability — that is worthy of, and welcoming for, Christ. This isn't just our home, it's also Our Lord's home, and so we treat it — and one another — accordingly.

Strength for Your Spirit

> "Charity is the bond of brotherhood, the foundation of peace, the mainstay and security of unity, which is greater than both hope and faith, which excels both good works and martyrdom, which will abide with us always, eternal with God in the kingdom of heaven."
>
> — *St. Cyprian*

Strength for Your Family

1. Does your family value sharing mealtimes together? How can you emphasize its importance?
2. Which night(s) of the week will work for you as "family dinner night"? Or which day(s) can you plan to have lunch together?
3. What specific things can you do to bring more joy into daily life, especially during chore times?
4. How does your family live the five guiding stars of the Holy Family? How can you become better at it?

Strength for Your Soul

Prayer for Trust and Confidence in God's Mercy
O Lord,
We ask for a boundless confidence and trust in your divine mercy,
and the courage to accept the crosses and sufferings
which bring immense goodness to our souls and that of your Church.

Help us to love you with a pure and contrite heart and to humble ourselves beneath your Cross
as we climb the mountain of holiness, carrying our cross that leads to heavenly glory.
May we receive you with great faith and love in holy Communion,
and allow you to act in us as you desire for your greater glory.

O Jesus, most adorable Heart and eternal fountain of Divine Love,

may our prayer find favor before the Divine Majesty
    of your heavenly Father.
Amen.

— St. Pio of Pietrelcina

Chapter Three

ACCEPTANCE
APPLICATION

When Matt was eight and Monica was five, two of my children, they had a squabble over a picture of the Blessed Mother that Monica had colored in her coloring book. She thought she'd done a bang-up job, but Matt didn't share that opinion. Their voices in the next room were quickly escalating, and the fact that it was the voice of our little "Princess" that was louder and more ferocious told me something was up beyond the typical quit-bugging-me fight. I put down my work and went to the doorway to listen. Usually I let them resolve things for themselves — within reason and barring the infliction of bodily harm.

"Monica, you can't color the Blessed Mother all different colors like that!" Matt was screaming.

"Yes, I can!" sobbed Monica.

"Uh uh!" Matthew shot back. "You're supposed to make her face peach and her veil blue. That's the way it is in all the pictures."

"But Mom said I can color my coloring books any way I want to!" Monica answered, and stomped her foot on the floor.

It was time to come out of my hiding place, for clearly I'd been implicated.

"Mom, didn't you say I could color in my coloring book any way I want to?" Monica begged with great crystal tears streaming down her face.

I took the book from Monica's trembling little hand. I had to admit the Madonna did look a bit peculiar with her face striped with fuchsia, brown, crimson, frog green, and a variety of other indescribable colors.

"Mom, you told us we have to respect holy things," prodded Matthew. "Isn't it disrespectful to make the Blessed Mother's face all goofy like that?"

"It isn't goofy! She looks pretty that way!" insisted Monica.

They were both right. We need to respect holy things, *and* Monica could color in her coloring book anyway she wanted to. I forced them into a halfhearted compromise and left the room.

I often think of that childhood spat as our family navigates the day-to-day challenges of life, especially the main one: accepting one another as we are and for who we are regardless of how we like to color our Madonna. For as much as one needs to be able to do things in his or her own way, the other needs to be able to voice (charitably) a differing opinion. That's the pull and tug that makes living together as family so problematic and rewarding all at the same time. The key is learning how to accept one another unconditionally, and that requires heroic patience, great sacrifice, and genuine, mutual love. In this lies an extraordinary amount of blessing.

The flip side is that their innate stubbornness is the very same stubbornness that will keep them from being tossed to and fro by the detrimental and even sinister forces of our godless culture.

I wasn't surprised that Matt's first college major was art; he's both a talented artist and a keen art connoisseur. At first things went well, but slowly I could see dissatisfaction setting in. Then one day, he announced that he was changing his major from art to political science and criminal justice. He told me that one of the reasons he had switched majors was because it can be difficult to earn a living in a career as competitive and subjective as commercial art. But the final straw came when he was assigned to study contemporary works of art that were absolutely appalling and contrary to his Catholic faith.

"There is no way," he said, "that a crucifix resting in a glass of urine can ever be considered art. And I won't even tell you what they did to the image of the Blessed Virgin Mary. Mom, if that's what they do in art today, then it's not for me." As I listened, I had a flashback to the day he insisted that Monica could *not* multicolor her Madonna. It's that same righteousness and gumption that led him to realize he wasn't cut out to be an art major.

Living together in a family community means mixing personalities and characteristics, regardless of whether you have one child or a dozen. Mutual love is a warm, genuine, and effective love that passes through each heart and proves itself through deeds. Time and again as family we're called to bear everything in genuine love, and it's our love that gives us patience and strength in suffering.

This doesn't imply that everything in the Fenelon Clan abode is always harmonious; it's not. We have our struggles just like any other family, and sometimes we outright bug each other. That's to be expected. However, along with the certainty we'll occasionally (and on some days, frequently) annoy each other is the expectation that we also will accept each other. We acknowledge that the others are valuable human beings, children of God, worthy of love and respect, with the Spirit dwelling in their souls. We allow them to be who they are and to act as they are called according to God's will. We also take into account all of the weaknesses and imperfections caused by original sin. We give them leeway for making mistakes, credit for gifts and accomplishments, and the room to be different from ourselves without judgment or criticism. That's acceptance.

We don't, however, look past sin. Sin is sin, and it offends God whether it's committed in the macrocosm of society or in the microcosm of the family. Of course, we know that we must admit and seek forgiveness for our own sins, particularly in the Sacrament of Reconciliation. If the words or actions within our families lead to sin, we're obligated to say or do something about it, keeping in mind that we, too, commit sin. Jesus warns against this kind of one-sidedness:

> "Or how can you say to your brother, 'Brother, let me take out the speck that is in your eye' when you yourself do not see the log that is in your own eye? You hypocrite, first take the log out of your own eye, and then you will see clearly to take out the speck that is in your brother's eye" (Lk 6:42).

Charitable admonishment, given in genuine love and sacrificial patience can move hearts away from sin and toward God. Of course, we have to be careful about taking two or three others with us when we go to discuss things with our brother, as it could quickly turn into a family feud. We don't want to gang up on anyone; rather, we want to present the situation as an item of concern to the entire family, first, because it affects everyone in the home

WHEN OTHERS SIN

"If your brother sins against you, go and tell him his fault, between you and him alone. If he listens to you, you have gained your brother. But if he does not listen, take one or two others along with you, that every word may be confirmed by the evidence of two or three witnesses. If he refuses to listen to them, tell it to the church; and if he refuses to listen even to the church, let him be to you as a Gentile and a tax collector."

— *Matthew 18:15-18*

and, second, because we care deeply about the person who has committed sin.

People falsely assume that anger is bad. It's only bad when it becomes destructive; constructive anger can be good. Think of Our Lord with the money-changers in the Temple. They were turning his Father's house into a den of thieves, cheating and deceiving the people (see Mt 21:12). Of course he was angry! It's how we express that emotion that makes anger destructive or constructive. When we admonish one another, do it without personal criticism and scathing accusations.

Word choice can have tremendous impact. We all know the volatile state of affairs between the pro-life movement and the pro-abortion initiative. Consider the difference between the images that come to mind when we say, "The anti-abortion protesters shoved their way to the front of the crowd, flinging hostile comments at the congressman" versus "The pro-life protesters made their way to the front of the crowd, voicing their alarm at the congressman's voting record." We need to be just as careful with our word choices in our families.

Discussing unpleasant things can be … well … unpleasant. Still, it has to be done for the sake of the holiness and harmony of the family. Mark and I encouraged open discussion whenever we sensed disgruntlement between family members (with a firm warning for anyone not involved to keep their noses out). Please note that I said "open discussion" and not whining, complaining, threatening, or mudslinging.

We also enforced the "First Person Pronoun Rule," which says we may only express ourselves using the first person pronoun ("I") as the subject of the sentence. We attached an article to our law. The words "hate you" may never follow the word "I." Period.

Basically, it works like this. When you're forced to use the first person pronoun, it makes it nearly impossible to fling insults and accusations at the other person. So, for instance, if Little Brother messed around in Big Brother's dresser drawers, Big Brother may only talk about it from a personal perspective. He can say, "I feel as though my privacy has been invaded and my trust in you was broken when you went through my dresser." He may not say, "You little creep, I'm going to beat the heck out of you because you messed up my stuff." The same applies to the other family relationships. A parent can say, "I feel as though my authority is being resisted when you don't follow through on the things I ask of you." A parent cannot say, "You stupid brat, why don't you do what I tell you?" A husband can say, "I was thoroughly embarrassed when I overheard you talking negatively about me to your friends. That really hurt." He cannot say, "You have a really big mouth, and you tick me off." Get the idea?

Our Lord himself set the standard:

"But I say to you that hear, Love your enemies, do good to those who hate you, bless those who curse you, pray for those who abuse you. To him who strikes you on the cheek, offer the other also; and from him who takes away your cloak do not withhold your coat as well. Give to every one who begs from you; and of him who takes away your goods do not ask them again. And as you wish that men would do to you, do so to them" (Lk 6:27-31).

I doubt our kids would automatically take to the "strikes you on the cheek" part, but with diligence and determination, we can open their hearts to at least considering it. If they, and indeed we ourselves as spouses and parents, can truly treat others as we would like to be treated, then we'll be on the road toward living in the spirit of sacrificial patience and genuine, mutual love.

Strength for Your Spirit

"Spread love everywhere you go: first of all in your own house. Give love to your children, to your wife or husband, to a next-door neighbor.... Let no one ever come to you without leaving better and happier. Be the living expression of God's kindness; kindness in your face, kindness in your eyes, kindness in your smile, kindness in your warm greeting."

— *Blessed Teresa of Calcutta*

Strength for Your Family

1. How do you voice your opinions to one another? Do you accept them or try to shut them out?
2. Do you have the courage to charitably draw attention to one another's sins? If not, why not?
3. What is your attitude toward anger? How do you express it?
4. What ground rules can you form for the discussion of difficult subjects (anger, sin, differing opinions, and so on)?

Strength for Your Soul

Prayer for Patience and Gentleness

Bestow on me, O Lord, a genial spirit and unwearied forbearance;
a mild, loving, patient, heart;
kindly looks, pleasant cordial speech, and manners
in the exchange of daily life;
that I may give offence to none,
but as much as in me lies live in charity with all men.
Amen.

— Johann Arndt (1555-1621)

Chapter Four

ABSOLUTELY POSITIVELY

Years ago, I got a refrigerator magnet from the YMCA that listed "101 Ways to Praise Your Child." (A *big* magnet with *small* type.) On it were the usual responses that parents give to their children when they've done something well, such as "Good job," "Way to go," or "Awesome." Some of them, however, were phrases that we might not think to say, like "I trust you," "You mean a lot to me," or "I respect you." How would our child's self-concept be affected if we resolved to use one of these little phrases in conversation with them each day?

I remember the last Christmas we had together before my dad died. That Christmas Eve after midnight Mass, we all sat around the table chatting. I don't know whether or not Dad had any clue that he would soon die, but there obviously was something on his mind and heart, and his mood was strangely reflective. He told us that, if he were to die that night, he wouldn't have to worry one bit about us four kids because he knew we had what it takes to make it in life. When you consider that my brother — the oldest — was twenty-six, my sisters were twenty-four and twenty-two, and I was a mere fifteen years old, this was an extraordinary thing to say. After that, he told each of us what gifts and talents he saw in him or her. You can imagine that what he said sunk deeply into our hearts. More than three decades later, we all clearly remember that night and even more clearly remember Dad's words of confidence in us. Not a day goes by when I don't stop for at least a moment to recall how Dad's description of my "moxie" has carried me through many tough times. That is how vastly impactful a parent's words of praise and acceptance to a child can be!

Complimenting our children doesn't have to be a sit-down-at-the-dining-room-table affair. In fact, if it's not done in a natural and unobtrusive way, it could freak them out. Also, whatever we say must be truthful, or we'll be teaching our kids how to be liars and schmoozers. In the "old days," we tucked notes into their lunchboxes. We still can, but now we have also technology at our fingertips, and so we can text, e-mail, voice mail, or instant message them. Then, too, a hug, pat on the back, jovial nudge, or playful hair tousling can speak volumes.

Not only should we speak words of praise and acceptance *to* a child, but also *about* a child. Whenever possible, Mark and I mention the positive qualities of one sibling to another. We do it in those little "teaching moments" that pop up every now and then, and it goes a long way in creating goodwill and mutual appreciation.

For example, our youngest son, John, is a capable fish keeper. He's bred them, raised them, and arranged his fish tank in wonderfully aesthetic ways. His knack for fish could easily be overlooked as "kid stuff," but I've used it as an example to his siblings as evidence of his gentleness, aptitude for nature, and love for God's creation. If they become irked over his fish equipment lying around, I remind them of how beautiful John's fish are to watch and what an important part of his development fish-keeping has become. When I talk to John about his fish, I point out

A COMMON PATH

"The family ... is a path common to all, yet one that is particular, unique, and unrepeatable, just as every individual is unrepeatable; it is a path from which man cannot withdraw. Indeed, a person normally comes into the world within the family and can be said to owe family the very fact of his existing as an individual. When he has no family, the person coming into the world develops an anguished sense of pain and loss, one that will subsequently burden his whole life."

— Blessed John Paul II, Letter to Families
for the International Year of the Family,
Gratissimam Sane, *February 2, 1994*

to him that his patience through the breeding process shows that he's growing in maturity and dependability.

It's good for families to celebrate the accomplishments of one another because it points out the reality that "I am who I am because of my connectedness with you." Of course, a job well done is a job well done, and it deserves credit. On the other hand, we have to be careful not to hold up the accomplishments of one child above the accomplishments of the others. This is an easy trap to slip into and a tough one to escape.

Our soldier-son's deployments garnered an awful lot of attention for him. Mark and I were partly responsible for that because we consistently petitioned relatives and friends for prayers while he was overseas. It could have seemed as though Matt was the only one of our children accomplishing anything of any worth, and that couldn't have been farther from the truth! Matt was especially the one to point this out, and he never wanted to be held up as a hero, especially not to his siblings.

While we weren't about to downplay the sacrifice Matt was making in serving his country, we also weren't about to dismiss the parallel accomplishments of his siblings. We made the most of all of them; Matt was doing great things in the Middle East, and his siblings were doing great things on U.S. soil.

This is even more important when there's distance between siblings. When Monica was between two and five years old, we changed her nickname from "Princess" to "Princess-grump-a-lot" because she suddenly became introverted and grumpy, especially toward her older brother. Every kindness Matt offered her was met with a rebuke. Mark and I were completely puzzled and felt entirely helpless. It's normal for relationships to vacillate between stages of closeness and distance, but as parents we have to guard against its getting out of hand. We did our best to bring Monica's finer qualities to Matt's attention. Sadly, it didn't mean a hill of beans to a rejected older brother. What were we to do? Out of sheer desperation, we observed the two together and jumped on every opportunity to show Matt the things that Monica did that were … less grumpy. In the meantime, we paid special attention to Monica and complimented her every time she seemed even remotely cheerful, especially toward Matt.

Sometimes we were convinced that it would've been much easier just to separate the two. But we didn't, and we're certainly glad we didn't. Monica came out of her grumpiness, Matt learned to better tolerate her moodiness, and the two of them began trusting each other again. Eventually, they became the best of friends.

Adult children run into the same types of difficulties and distances that young children do. Although they're more mature, they're also more stubborn. While we refrain from interfering unless it's something critical, we do step in for as long as it takes to draw attention to the good qualities of each sibling and to remind them of the things that they deep-down love about one another. Mark and I believe that family is forever — Fenelon Clan doesn't dissolve when the last child moves out of the house. The children will still be Fenelon Clan even though they'll have joined new "clans" through their God-given vocations and relationships. They'll need each other more than ever then — especially after Mark and I are gone. What they learn now as a nuclear family will carry them through in the future.

Strength for Your Spirit

> "The Church ... knows well the fundamental role which the family is called upon to play. Furthermore, she knows that a person goes forth from the family in order to realize in a new family unit his particular vocation in life. Even if someone chooses to remain single, the family continues to be, as it were, his existential horizon, that fundamental community in which the whole network of social relations is grounded, from the closest and most immediate to the most distant. Do we not often speak of the 'human family' when referring to all the people living in the world?"

> — *Blessed John Paul II, Letter to Families*
> *for the International Year of the Family,*
> Gratissimam Sane, *February 2, 1994*

Strength for Your Family

1. Think of five new phrases you can use to give positive feedback to another family member.
2. How can you remind yourselves of the accomplishments and good qualities of each family member?
3. How do you react when there's distance between siblings? What can you do to balance it?

Strength for Your Soul

Prayer for Baptized Children

Lord Jesus Christ,
you loved children so much that you said:
"Whoever welcomes a child welcomes me."
Hear our prayers and, with your unfailing protection,
watch over these children (this child)
whom you have blessed with the grace of baptism.
When they (he/she) have (has) grown to maturity,
grant that they (he/she) will confess your name in
    willing faith,
be fervent in charity,
and persevere courageously in the hope of reaching
    your kingdom,
where you live and reign forever and ever.
Amen.

Prayer for a Child Not Yet Baptized

All-powerful God and Father,
you are the source of all blessings, the protector of
    infants,
whose gift of children enriches and brightens a mar-
    riage.

Look with favor on this child
and, when he/she is reborn of water and the Holy
   Spirit,
bring him/her into your own spiritual family, the
   Church,
there to become a sharer in your kingdom
and with us to bless your name forever.
We ask this through Christ our Lord.
Amen.

> — *United States Conference of Catholic Bishops,*
> Catholic Household Blessings & Prayers,
> Revised Edition

Chapter Five

GOOD TIMES AND BAD

When Mark lost his job after twenty-one years of service to a nonprofit organization, it was a devastating blow for our family. The organization was downsizing and decided to dismantle its in-house print shop, of which he was the manager. That was basically the only job he'd ever known during our entire married life, and the prospect of starting all over again was frightening. It was compounded by the fact that four out of our six family members have chronic illnesses, and so adequate health insurance is an absolute necessity.

We tried to keep the kids out of worry's way, but weren't completely successful. Tensions were high, and it was like walking a tightrope without a safety net. In spite of that, we rallied around Mark, assured him of our confidence in his resourcefulness and abilities, and used every opportunity to boost morale — both his and ours.

Additionally, we tried to accentuate the resourcefulness of each family member so that we could pull together as a cohesive, purposeful unit. We had to focus on what was good in our lives so that we could keep moving in a positive direction. First and foremost, that included each other. This was a crucial time for encouraging each one to do whatever he or she could to help the family and to practice sacrificial patience!

We can learn a lot about this from St. Thérèse of Lisieux. A nun in her community was a source of constant annoyance for her. It seems all she could see were the woman's disagreeable traits. She knew, of course, that these were dangerous feelings to harbor, so she resolved, by the grace of God, to treat this sister as if she were her most cherished friend. Whenever she met her, she prayed for her and at the same time offered to God the sister's virtues and good qualities. Still, she wasn't satisfied with merely praying for this nun, so she began to serve her in every way she could. Rather than give a disagreeable answer, she quickly changed the subject. When the temptation was particularly violent, she would slip away without any suspicion on the part of the sister. Finally, the sister said to St. Thérèse: "Tell me, Sister Thérèse, what is it that attracts you to me so strongly? I never meet you without being welcomed with your most gracious smile!" Imagine what this kind of resolve could do for our families!

If we judged by the images of the Holy Family on Christmas cards, we'd think they lived in total placidity. Perhaps they did at times, but likely their lives were speckled with disharmonies as well. Did St. Joseph make his decision to quietly divorce, and then in turn not divorce, Mary without any struggle? At the same time, our Blessed Mother was tending to her cousin Elizabeth as she waited for St. Joseph to make his decision, wondering if he would ever again trust her, contemplating the possibility of being stoned to death, and trying to figure out what would happen to the Child within her womb should St. Joseph abandon her. Then Jesus came, and with him came tremendous joy, but also some really tight spots. How did they handle having to suddenly pull up roots and flee to Egypt? We know that both St. Joseph and the Blessed Mother followed God's will above all things. But as human beings, they also had free will and separate intellects, which meant that their interpretation of how to fulfill God's will could have been very different. As the woman of the house, the Blessed Mother would have had to let St. Joseph take the lead, and this meant being patient and allowing him to figure things out in his own way. As the man of the house, St. Joseph would have had to let the Blessed Mother take charge of the domestic issues involved, and this meant being patient and allowing her to figure things out in her own way.

Think, too, of the complexity of their daily life. St. Joseph, although head of the family, was actually the lowliest of the three: He was just a man, while Jesus was God and the Blessed Mother was born without original sin. Nevertheless, the Blessed Mother, although Queen of the Universe, was for all practical purposes a simple housewife and bound to submissiveness to her husband and service to her son. Jesus, the King of Kings, experienced all the frailties of the human condition while at the same time having the ability to rise above them. In spite of their "celebrity status," the Holy Family lived simply and inconspicuously, waiting patiently upon each other and loving one another completely and unconditionally.

We know our Blessed Mother's love is pure, deep, and comprehensive, and we can be sure that St. Joseph and Our Lord shared in that same love. Hers was both a supernatural and a natural love that knew no limits. From that limitless love sprang limitless patience and acceptance.

There's an adage that says we become similar to the object of our love. The upside of that is that when we love God, we become more like him. The upside of loving our

THE LOVE OF MARY

"Mary is a woman who loves. How could it be otherwise? As a believer who in faith thinks with God's thoughts and wills with God's will, she cannot fail to be a woman who loves. We sense this in her quiet gestures, as recounted by the infancy narratives in the Gospel. We see it in the delicacy with which she recognizes the need of the spouses at Cana and makes it known to Jesus. We see it in the humility with which she recedes into the background during Jesus' public life, knowing that the Son must establish a new family and that the Mother's hour will come only with the Cross, which will be Jesus' true hour. When the disciples flee, Mary will remain beneath the Cross; later, at the hour of Pentecost, it will be they who gather around her as they wait for the Holy Spirit."

— *Pope Benedict XVI, Deus Caritas Est, 41*

family members is that we become more like them. Have you ever seen a married couple celebrating their fiftieth wedding anniversary who actually look alike? When we truly love and are patient with one another, it becomes contagious, and we naturally begin to accept one another — blemishes and all.

Strength for Your Spirit

"Our entire life is a great hymn of praise to God's infinite love. A great hymn of praise! Everything that we bear and endure, that we experience in happy hours, in hardships and trials, everything, everything becomes somehow a stanza in that great, great hymn to the honor, to the glory of the eternal, infinite God."

— Father Joseph Kentenich, Servant of God
and Founder of the Schoenstatt Apostolic Movement

Strength for Your Family

1. What is the worst crisis you've ever faced as a couple? as a family?
2. How did you handle it?
3. How were you blessed through it?
4. What would you do again and what would you like to do better in the case that you face another such crisis?

Strength for Your Soul

Prayer of St. Gianna

Jesus,

I promise you to submit myself to all that tou permit to befall me, make me only know your will. My most sweet Jesus, infinitely merciful God, most tender Father of souls, and in a particular way of the most weak, most miserable, most infirm which you carry with special tenderness between your divine arms, I come to you to ask you, through the love and merits of your Sacred Heart, the grace to comprehend and to do always your holy will, the grace to confide in you, the grace to rest securely through time and eternity in your loving divine arms.

— St. Gianna Beretta Molla

Chapter Six

PUSHING THE LIMIT

Certainly we have to accept our children for who they are, but we're also responsible for helping them become the "who" God wants them to be. In that respect, our job is to provide the framework in which they can grow, develop, mature, and find their godly path in life. This includes the less-fun part of parenting: setting limits. Even tougher is watching those limits get pushed. Wise parents know that the minute we set a limit, our kids will push it. Look what happened to Adam and Eve. God told them not to eat of the tree of the knowledge of good and evil, or they would die. What did they do? They turned right around and ate from it anyway (see Gn 2:17). That was under threat of *death*! So, you don't think our kids are going to pull the same thing? Of course they are.

We don't set limits just to antagonize our children, although they might think so. We set limits in order to steer them away from physical and spiritual danger and toward God. One of the greatest dangers we face today — not only for our children but also for us — is technology.

From the beginning, Mark and I had fought the new technology of cell phones and text messaging. We saw them as impersonal and addictive. Slowly, we caved in and got cell phones ourselves. It wasn't long after that we found ourselves texting just like our kids.

I would still argue that text messaging can be impersonal and addictive, and I fear what it will do to our grammar and spelling (or lack thereof) as a society, but I've discovered that there are certain advantages to having that technology accessible, especially to busy moms of older kids.

With two already out of the house and the third standing in the doorway, it's become more and more of a challenge to maintain contact with my adult children. So I text them.

I send a variety of "checking up" messages, like, "How're you doing?", "How was your exam?", "I took you to Mass with me today!", "Feeling better?", "I love you!", and "I miss you!" I'll also send a reminder on feast days, holy days of obligation, and Fenelon Clan events. Occasionally, I'll send a humorous little quip or riotous family memory just to give them something to chuckle about. If they're doing well in general, I'll make sure to check up on them once a week. If they're ill or under particular stress, I'll do it a couple of times a week or even daily until the situation improves. Sometimes they send a message to me about something private they can't speak about aloud because of where they are or who's around.

Of course, texting can't take the place of genuine human contact, but I've found that it isn't the huge, devouring monster I once thought it was if one keeps it in check.

This is the challenge we face in setting limits and teaching our children prudent use of new technologies. Technological advancement is here, whether we like it or not, and technology will continue to advance regardless of how we try to fight it. It would be irresponsible for us to throw up our hands and let the chips fall where they may, so to speak, giving in to every request from our children for this or that new gizmo. On the other hand, we mustn't be fearful and overly restrictive. That will only serve to do one of two things. Either our children also will become fearful of new things, or they'll develop an insatiable appetite for them.

The first step is to make sure that we've set appropriate limits for ourselves. If we're racing out to get every new device, if we're spending hours in front of the computer, if we don't have our own inclinations in check, how can we possibly expect our children to do so? If we want our children to conquer something, we must first conquer it ourselves.

Once we have a handle — or at least are striving to get a handle — on our own use of technology, we can begin to help our children get a handle on theirs. This begins when they're small. Young children need reasonable limits for everything they do, but at the same time need to be given the opportunity to make their own choices whenever possible.

For example, Mark and I didn't want our children watching excessive amounts of television. We told them they had one hour per day, but we gave them the choice between watching a television show or DVD that meets with our approval. Incidentally, there are scientific reasons to set limits on the amount of time we're in front of the electronic screens. A 2010 study conducted at the University of Bristol, United Kingdom, found that kids who spent more than two hours a day in front of the screen were 61 percent more likely than children with less screen time to have increased psychological difficulties (LifeSite-News.com, October 10, 2010).

For more years than I can even remember, we've had the tradition of "Family Movie Night," usually on Saturdays. Mark and I wanted to make this an evening to look forward to, and so we'd try to plan ahead by renting or borrowing a movie from the library and reminding the

Clan to keep Saturday night free. We'd have supper, clean up, and then move into the living room. When the kids were small, it was no problem to pile everyone on the couch. As they got older, it was more like packing a grocery bag, taking care to put the heavier stuff on the bottom and the lighter stuff on top and somehow fitting it all together efficiently.

The kids have always loved these nights because they thought that Mom and Dad were finally letting them have some "modern" entertainment. Mom and Dad have always loved it because our clandestine motive was to teach the kids how to make prudent choices in entertainment. We usually offered two or three movies, and let the kids choose which one they wanted to watch. As the kids got older, we let them pick out their own movies but set parameters for their choices. The parameters changed as the children got older, allowing for more adult subject matter as they were able to handle it. However, movies with vile language, unnecessary violence, and sexual innuendo are not allowed in our home. Even the over-18 kids don't push that limit because they know better. It's nonnegotiable.

Making informed decisions puts our kids in proactive rather than reactive mode and helps prepare them for making the more difficult and consequential decisions that will come later in life. This is a long-term process that takes time, patience, and perseverance. Additionally, we must be consistent. We can't leave our kids to themselves for years and years and then suddenly come down hard with a new set of rules — we're sure to get rebellion, not cooperation. Ultimately, we want our children to set their own limits for the use of technology.

Some parents convince themselves that a "little" technology won't hurt — and it won't if it is indeed a little. But most children aren't strong enough to resist the temptation to over use and even abuse digital devices. Once we place a gizmo in a child's hand, there's no going back; giving them a taste of it runs the risk of developing an insatiable craving. Before we take that step, we must be sure that the child's character is sufficiently developed.

Music players can be another addictive device that is detrimental to family life. Again, this depends on how and for how long they are used. Music in and of itself is a beautiful thing and can do a great deal of good for the mind and soul. Music that is aggressive or lewd is harmful, and we must be choosy about the types of songs that our kids listen to. MP3 players weren't around when our oldest kids were preteens, but our other two weren't allowed to have them until they reached their teenage years, and even then it was with limitations. Our kids are not allowed to be "plugged in" during family times. This includes family activities, mealtimes, and while riding in the car. They can listen while they're doing their own stuff and, depending upon the situation, probably during chore time.

In general, we've curtailed the use of any kind of technology if we sensed that it was causing a child to become distracted, moody, uncooperative, or ornery. We've observed one or all of these effects from time to time, and while we can't prove that technology was the cause, it was our gut feeling, and usually we ended up being right. Even if there was no apparent detriment, we've always advocated being completely screenless and noiseless for one hour each night before bedtime to quiet the soul and refocus the mind.

We consider hanging out with friends entertainment, too. Therefore, we also place limits upon it. We *want* our children to have friendships, but we want them to have friendships that are lasting and uplifting. This gets harder to do as they get older; eventually we have to let them choose their own friends for better or worse. That's why it's so important to help them evaluate, initiate, and receive appropriate friendship when they are young. Granted, sometimes things just slipped past us. Yet, we tried to observe the way our kids interacted with other kids and to help them find their footing, so to speak. For the kids who were less outgoing, we had to help them learn to be more assertive and stand their ground when they were not being treated considerately. Our kids who were more outgoing needed some training in consideration for others. Both sides of the coin required the setting of limits.

We've always enjoyed it when our kids invited their friends over; they have some wonderful friends, and we've been happy to know them. However, entertaining even the most wonderful of friends can lead to disaster without guidelines. The same limits regarding digital devices, televisions, DVD players, and computers apply to our kids when they are spending time with friends and to the friends themselves if they are in our home. One of our rules is that friends are not allowed in bedrooms. This rule is even more important when kids start dating, therefore we made the blanket rule: no friends in bedrooms. Our kids' first reaction was "You don't trust us." We do trust them. And we also trust the devil to use every trick in the book to tempt them. As Christians, we're obligated not only to avoid sin itself but also to avoid the near occasion of sin.

THE NEAR OCCASION OF SIN

As Father John Hardon explains in his wonderful *Modern Catholic Dictionary*, a near occasion of sin is "any person, place, or thing that of its nature or because of human frailty can lead one to do wrong, thereby committing sin." He goes on to explain, "If the danger is certain and probable, the occasion is proximate; if the danger is slight, the occasion becomes remote. It is voluntary if it can easily be avoided." And, he continues, "there is no obligation to avoid a remote occasion unless there is probable danger of its becoming proximate." On the other hand, "There is a positive obligation to avid a voluntary proximate occasion of sin even though the occasion of evildoing is due only to human weakness."

Since we're talking about our children's social lives, we also should talk about the "C" and "D" words: curfews and dating. The families we know run the spectrum. Some have negotiated curfews on a per-case basis, while others had preset curfews that were nonnegotiable under any circumstances. Fenelon Clan fell somewhere in between. We had a basic framework from which we operated, setting curfews based on the child's age and the circumstances. We've been blessed in that our children's cousins have been among their best friends, and our brothers- and sisters-in-law have morals and standards that are similar to ours. Additionally, our children were usually spending time either at our house or one of our siblings' houses, and it almost always involved a sleepover. Since they were in a safe environment physically and spiritually, we didn't worry.

It was a different story when they were out and about. In those cases, they had a definite time at which they had to be home, and there were certain places they could and could not go. They weren't allowed to hang out at the homes of friends when the parents were not there. They weren't allowed to wander around on the streets; they had to have a specific place and a purpose for their time with their friends. If they were considering a change in plans, we were to be consulted by phone first. Letting anyone else drive one of our cars was absolutely *verboten*. Before they left the house, we asked for at least a basic itinerary so that we would know where they'd be, and when and if they were going to miss curfew, we expected a phone call. A missed curfew without a phone call earned anywhere from a week to two weeks and up to a month of grounding, depending on the severity of the infraction.

For the most part, preteens were in by 9:30 in the evening unless they were at a function that lasted longer; in that case, they had to be either with us or with someone whom we knew and trusted. Younger teens were given a time anywhere between 10 and 10:30 and sometimes up to 11. Older teens could stay out until between 11 and midnight with an occasional 1 in the morning if it was for good reason. We didn't feel anyone had a good reason to be out after that. Once they were past age eighteen, we seldom had to worry about monitoring limits; the kids usually did this on their own. The limits broadened but weren't dropped as each child reached that age.

So far, our older children have chosen to live with us at home during their first years of college. We offered them a deal: if they lived at home while in school, they could have free room and board and I would do their laundry for them. We're careful not to breathe down their necks, but at the same time, we let them know that certain things were expected of them, and we hold them accountable for those expectations. We no longer need to know where they're going or what they're doing every time they leave the house, but we do need to have a general idea of when they're going and coming. There's a practical reason for this. Whoever is making meals needs to know how many people will be home to eat them. If we're planning an event, we need to know how many people will be around for it. These are all simple courtesies that are necessary for any living situation, whether it be with a family or housemates. Our requirements are meant to prepare them to be responsible adults who eventually will live with others in a home, convent, monastery, or rectory.

We can expect our kids to argue and resist curfew, at least occasionally. That's normal, and sometimes they actually have good reasons for questioning our decisions. However, we can't just cave in because we're sick of the arguing.

Which brings us to the "D" word. Again, we've seen families make a full range of decisions about dating. We've been accused by other parents and even some of our children's peers of being too rigid in our dating limits. Our kids, though, accepted them without trouble. Our rule is no dating whatsoever before the age of sixteen, and in mixed groups only until the age of eighteen. This doesn't mean that we secluded our kids and forbade them to get to know the opposite gender. Indeed, we encouraged them to participate in activities and form friendships with both boys and girls. We especially encouraged them to join service groups and other kinds of youth activities that would put them in contact with a variety of personalities of both genders. What we discouraged was pairing off before they were mature enough to handle it.

How do we gauge that maturity? It depends on the individual, but there are some generalities that apply to all children and teenagers. Some of this leads back to our discussion of limiting technology. Pop culture puts an enormous amount of pressure on our kids to become sexually intimate with others, even at very young ages.

Before our kids can enter into relationships on their own, they have to be mature enough to resist, or at least question, cultural trends, and the grave dangers they pose to our souls.

We have to consider — and discuss with our children — the real purpose for dating. It isn't about having a good time, although it certainly can be fun. It's about discerning a vocation and finding the person that God has intended for us from all eternity. That happens with discretion, not experimentation. If you aren't old enough to consider marriage, then you're not old enough to date one-on-one.

When our kids do begin to date seriously, we have a frank discussion with them about vigilance and propriety. Just because they're old enough to date doesn't mean they're immune from temptation. In fact, no one is immune from temptation regardless of age! We encourage them to take every precaution by refraining from behaviors such as lap-sitting, lounging in the dark, lying down together, staying out until the wee hours, and spending too much time alone together.

All couples need some time alone, especially if they're serious enough to be discerning marriage, so that they can truly get to know each other. But the behaviors mentioned above fling the door wide open for temptation. Even if the two don't "do" anything, placing themselves in the position — sometimes literally — in which they have to think about it is almost as bad as committing the sin itself. If we truly love God with all our heart, then we'll want our behavior to be impeccable at all times out of respect for him, for ourselves, and for the person we're dating.

Jesus explained this in his Sermon on the Mount, "You have heard that it was said, 'You shall not commit adultery.' But I say to you that every one who looks at a woman lustfully has already committed adultery with her in his heart" (Mt 5:27-28).

Our Lord's caution is true for all of us. Real, godly relationships work to uplift and enrich, not drag down and tempt. In order to do that, we have to limit ourselves before we sin, not after.

Strength for Your Spirit

> "This totality of *human and Christian virtues* which are proper to spouses who take on their mission before civil society and the Church, must be transmitted in the first place to the children. Furthermore, through a type of *osmosis*, the children absorb in their lives and personalities what they breathe in the family environment, which is the fruit of the virtues their parents have put into action in their own lives. The best means of impressing these virtues on children's hearts is to present them as engraved in their parent's life. Human virtues and Christian virtues, harmoniously and solidly united, make the ideal perceived by their parents desirable and stimulate children to undertake their acquisition."

— Blessed John Paul II, "Parents Are the First and Primary Educators of Their Children," Discourse to the Participants of the Plenary Assemblies of the Pontifical Council for the Family, October 10, 1986

Strength for Your Family

1. How do you use technology? For yourself? In your home? Is it done in purity and prudence? If not, what can you do to change it?
2. What is your decision-making process? Is it working for you, or does it need to be changed? How?
3. Does your family have designated quiet times? What steps can you take to secure at least one quiet time a week?
4. What are your policies on curfews and dating? Do they need adjustment?

Strength for Your Soul

A Prayer of Hopeful Surrender
O my God,
I want to base my hope in you alone.
Since you can do everything,
deign to bring to birth in my soul
the virtue I desire.
To obtain this grace of your infinite
mercy I will very often repeat:
O Jesus, gentle and humble of heart,
make my heart like yours!
Amen.

— St. Thérèse of Lisieux

Chapter Seven

CONSEQUENCES, NATURALLY

M ark and I don't force our kids to participate in family activities because, in the end, it only fosters resentment and disharmony. On the other hand, some things are absolutes. Until the kids enter college, we require them to attend Mass with the family. According to the precepts of the Catholic Church, they have to attend anyway, so they might as well attend with us.

Additionally, Sundays are reserved for family. From the time the kids were little, Sunday brunch and supper were important family events, and we all went out of our way to be together at those times. When the kids started holding jobs, we asked them to do everything possible not to work on Sundays, realizing that sometimes there's no way around it. If they did have to work, we asked that they try to be around for at least brunch or supper. The kids weren't allowed to hang out with friends on Sundays; exceptions were rare. Meetings, youth activities, and social events were out of the question unless their attendance was essential. Unless we were cornered into it, we didn't run errands or go shopping on Sundays either. Mark and I put the same limits on ourselves, even though it hasn't always been easy. However, we've done our best to keep Sunday free for the family and voiced our preference not to schedule Sunday meetings or activities. The rules are "bent" if the entire family attends together — as long as it's done in unity and respect for the Lord's Day.

Work was another story. Both Mark and I are self-employed, which means if there is a pressing deadline or demanding project, there's no one to take our places. Sometimes we just have to work on Sundays. When that happens, we've tried to slip the work in between the most important family times: Mass, brunch, and supper. Mark has made exceptional sacrifices in this regard, often working around the clock toward the end of the week just to free up time for the family on Sundays. Our example has paid off because we see our kids, even the ones no longer living at home, strive to be with the family on Sundays, at least for a while.

We also work hard at assuring that our "Sunday attitude" flows into the weekdays. We promote the same respect for God and family unity throughout the week, using the Ten Commandments as our baseline, in the hopes that through our efforts our children will experience the love of God firsthand.

EXPERIENCING THE LOVE OF GOD

"The young must find in their own families the normal place in which to grow humanly and spiritually. I therefore hope that families will always be true centers of evangelization where each one can experience the love of God that may then be communicated to others and first of all to children."

— Pope Benedict XVI, To the Bishops of the Episcopal Council of Laos and Cambodia, June 9, 2007

In the early years, when we listened to every expert there was except our own, sensible guts, Mark and I used spanking and squatting as punishment for misbehavior. Squatting was a practice I'd learned about from a schoolteacher neighbor who worked at a facility in an extremely rough neighborhood. Since the teachers weren't allowed to touch the kids when they caused trouble, they had them squat on their haunches in a corner of the room or along the playground fence.

It was a miserable failure, and eventually we gave it up. We found natural consequences to be the most effective form of correction. When we make a mistake, we fix it, don't we? Misbehavior is merely a mistake in deciding how to behave; therefore, we fix it. If a child has offended a sibling, he makes up for it. If a child fails to obey his parents, he loses privileges. If a child neglects his duties, he loses free time and must complete them before he does anything else.

It was Luke's job to sweep the wood floors during chore time, and he had bypassed our utility closet for weeks in a row thinking that I would never notice. I did. One day I had had enough and told him that he had to completely empty out the closet and sweep it clean from corner to corner before he was allowed to continue his day. Grudgingly, he set to work. A few minutes later, I heard him screaming and ran to see what was wrong.

He was standing in the hallway with a horrified look on his face.

"What's wrong?" I demanded.

"There! There!" he screamed again. He pointed to something in the corner. "That's disgusting!"

It was a dead mouse, flattened and positioned as if it had been there for a while.

"You see! I told you! That's what you get for skipping the closet all those weeks!" I yelled at him. Without an ounce of sympathy, I made him scoop up the mouse and carry it out to the alley garbage can.

When Mark got home, Luke painfully told his story. Much to our amazement, Mark burst out laughing: "Oh, man! That's the mouse I killed last night while I was working on the house. I killed it with the broom, and forgot to pick it up because I was in the middle of a project."

Regardless of where the mouse came from, Luke learned a valuable lesson; he never skipped the closet floor again.

The key to correcting our kids' behavior is to be firm enough to drive home our point but controlled enough to not beat them over the heads — figuratively or literally. Our job is to effectively usher them into adulthood — a deliberate, gradual process that begins at birth and continues for most of their lives. We give our children more autonomy beginning at age fifteen or sixteen — depending on the personality — and continue until they prove to us that they can handle things on their own. This doesn't necessarily occur at eighteen years of age. We've had kids try to pull the "I'm an adult now" line on us, and our response has always been, "When you start acting like one, you'll be treated like one." That pretty much stops the argument. Also, maturity isn't a straight-line progression; it's more like two steps forward and a step back here and there. Eventually, they'll find their way if we do our job as parents in setting appropriate limits and teaching them natural consequences that are respectful of their needs as individuals.

Strength for Your Spirit

"Therefore conscience is more to be obeyed than authority imposed from outside. For conscience obliges in virtue of divine command, whether written down in a code or instilled by natural law. To weigh conscience in the scales against obedience to legal authority is to compare the weight of divine and human decrees. The first obliges more than the second, and sometimes against the second."

— St. Thomas Aquinas,
Disputations Concerning Truth

Strength for Your Family

1. What is your main objective in disciplining your children?
2. What is your primary means of discipline?
3. Is it effective? Why or why not?

Strength for Your Soul

Prayer of St. Francis before the Crucifix
Most High, Glorious God,
enlighten the darkness of my heart,
and give me correct faith,
sure hope and perfect charity,
with understanding and knowledge, Lord,
so that I may fulfill your holy and true command.
Amen.

— St. Francis of Assisi

Chapter Eight

LORD, HEAR OUR PRAYER!

I was in the emergency room one night, doing what most parents do at least a few times in their lives — bringing in a kid who decided to get seriously ill after the doctor's office and urgent care center had closed. Of course, it was Friday. Then I did another thing most parents do at least a few times in their lives — realized that I was in such a rush to get the sick kid into a doctor's hands that I had neglected my own needs.

Once Luke was under medical staff care, I excused myself. As I walked through the waiting area toward the restroom, I saw a remarkable sight. There was a family sitting in the center of the room, huddled together with their heads bowed, holding hands and praying out loud for their loved one! I was so touched that tears came to my eyes. Rather than disturb them, I kept walking. On my way back to Luke's cubicle, I noticed they'd finished praying, and so I stopped to talk to them.

"Are you the family who was praying together?" I asked. Their eyes widened, and they looked at one another. Likely they thought I was going to berate them for a public display of Christianity.

"Uh, yes, we are," one of the older women answered with startled hesitation.

"Well, thank you. That's one of the most beautiful things I've ever seen and a real witness to our Christian faith. May God bless you and may your loved one soon be well," I said.

"Well, thank *you!*" she responded, breaking into a weary smile.

I've always thought Fenelon Clan was a prayerful family, but this waiting-room family got me to thinking about how we could do better. This family wasn't putting on a show; they were in need and reached out to the heavenly Father for help. Their surroundings didn't matter — they did what came naturally to them, and it was obvious that prayer was part of their daily life.

Is prayer part of our daily lives? Is it so natural to us that we could break out in prayer anytime, anywhere? I asked myself these questions. Perhaps we don't have the personality to spontaneously pray aloud in a public place, even in a crisis. But to at least pray — to have God as our primary thought in every situation — is what the First Commandment requires of us.

Prayer is far more than begging God for what we want. In prayer, we acknowledge God's power and goodness and admit our own neediness and dependence on him. When we pray, we express our faith and hope in God. Through prayer, we obtain grace and elevate our minds and hearts to a greater knowledge and love of God. The more we pray, the more we come to know and love him. It's like exercising — at first it's a real pain (often literally) to fit it into our hectic schedules. Once we push ourselves to get started, we start to see and feel the benefits. The more we exercise, the more efficient our minds and the stronger our bodies become. Eventually, exercise becomes a natural part of our routine, and we do it without even giving it a second thought. So, too, with prayer.

There's nothing inherently wrong in asking God for things; indeed, we should, because he's both our Creator and Father. When we only ask of him, though, we forge a very self-centered relationship with him. God is a good and loving Father, and we should show him our love in every way possible. The most obvious sign of our love for God is prayer. Every truly good prayer contains not only petitions and expressions of sorrow for our failures, but also praise and adoration of God. What would it be like if our kids only came to us when they wanted something? Eventually we'd feel like we just were being used. Our enthusiasm would cool, and we might even get to the point of dreading our kids' approach. God won't ever lose his enthusiasm for us and will never dread our approach, but if we only go to him to get something out of him, our relationship with him will lack a critical dimension, and our enthusiasm will cool. There are two sides to every coin; in the same way, there are two sides to every prayer. Prayer isn't just about speaking, it's also about listening.

We could read a multitude of books on prayer, and there are many excellent ones out there, but we can get a "quick start" lesson in prayer from the Our Father. It's the perfect prayer because Our Lord taught it to us and because it contains all the essential elements of prayer. St. Thérèse of Lisieux used to meditate on it for hours at a time, contemplating the individual words one by one and letting them sink into her mind and heart. Our kids might not be able to sit still during an entire St. Thérèse-style examination of the Our Father, but meditating on the prayer line by line, or breaking it up into a study over many days, would be a great place to start.

We've prayed the Rosary together to greater and lesser success over the years. There are no hard-and-fast rules for when and how to pray the Rosary; each family

FAMILY PRAYER AND THE ROSARY

"A similar need for commitment and prayer arises in relation to another critical contemporary issue: the family, the primary cell of society, increasingly menaced by forces of disintegration on both the ideological and practical planes, so as to make us fear for the future of this fundamental and indispensable institution and, with it, for the future of society as a whole. The revival of the Rosary in Christian families, within the context of a broader pastoral ministry to the family, will be an effective aid to countering the devastating effects of this crisis typical of our age."

— *Blessed John Paul II,* Rosarium Virginis Mariae, 6

has to find its own style and rhythm. This is true of family prayer in general. What works wonderfully for one family may end up being a complete disaster for another. Flexibility and understanding can make the difference between our kids dreading family prayer or looking forward to it.

Like any good habit, prayer requires frequent reminders. If we want to remember our annual checkup with the doctor, we write a sticky note to ourselves and hang it in a conspicuous spot so we'll be sure to see it. God is the best healer there is, and we don't want to miss a single appointment with him. So, we "hang" reminders around our house called sacramentals.

Sacramentals are signs and symbols that draw us closer to God. Holy water, the Sign of the Cross, blessings, blessed rosaries, and crucifixes are examples of sacramentals. They're like spiritual sticky notes that act as reminders to us of God and his goodness.

A blessed rosary hangs from the shelf next to my computer monitor. It was a special gift to me from my Schoenstatt community, and I treasure it. The crucifix is an unusual one — the Blessed Mother stands beneath Our Lord holding a chalice that captures the Precious Blood as it pours from Jesus' side. Whenever I find myself ready to tear my hair out over a pressing deadline or project that just won't seem to come together, I stop, take a deep breath (even though it's in between seething words), and meditate for a second or two on that crucifix. I imagine myself in the place of our Lady, holding the chalice and grieving over her suffering Son and the Blood as a representation of the words he wishes me to write that will convey his tremendous love for mankind. If I didn't have the crucifix within sight as I work, I likely wouldn't be drawn into such a meditation when my writing runs amok.

I once heard a homily in which the priest ever so beautifully explained why Catholics have holy pictures and statues in their churches. "When a loved one dies," he said, "we want to keep their memory fresh in our mind, and we want to feel close to them again because we love and miss them. So we get a favorite picture of them, give it a nice frame, and put it on our desk or dresser so they'll 'always be right there with us.'" Then he went on to say that the Triune God, our Blessed Mother, St. Joseph, and all the other saints also are our loved ones and we want to feel close to them. So, we place their images where we'll see them, and they'll "always be right there with us."

Strength for Your Spirit

"People who only know how to think about God during certain fixed periods of the day will never get very far in the spiritual life. In fact, they will not even think of him in the moments they have religiously marked off for 'mental prayer.'"

— Thomas Merton, Seeds of Contemplation

Strength for Your Family

1. What does your family prayer time look like?
2. How can you make it more fruitful?
3. How can you come to a deeper understanding and appreciation of the Rosary?
4. What form of prayer works best for your family? How can you capitalize on that in order to help your children foster a more animated relationship with God?

Strength for Your Soul

A Prayer of Thanksgiving for the Family

We bless your name, O Lord,
for sending your own incarnate Son,
to become part of a family,
so that, as he lived its life,
he would have experienced its worries and its joys.
We ask you, Lord,
to protect and watch over this family,
so that in the strength of your grace
its members may enjoy prosperity,
and, as the Church alive in the home,
bear witness in this world to your glory.
We ask this through Christ our Lord. Amen.

— United States Conference of Catholic Bishops,
Catholic Household Blessings & Prayers,
Revised Edition

Chapter Nine

CHURCH IN MINIATURE

What's true for churches also is true for our homes. This is why the Catholic Church refers to the family as the "domestic church." As domestic church, our family forms a community of believers. Like the early Christians, we gather in our home to praise God and support one another. We're a microcosm of the larger Church, and as such we strive to incorporate the traditions and practices of the Faith into our daily lives.

It's good to have sacramentals that remind us *to* pray, but it's even better to have a place in our home in which we *can* pray. The setup doesn't have to be extravagant; we're not building a cathedral, we're building a domestic church! A small corner will do, with a shelf or cabinet to hold religious items — whatever is meaningful to us and fosters a prayerful disposition. That could be anything from a crucifix, holy water, and a prayer book to an array of holy pictures, candles, and statues. We might even want to have our prayer corner blessed by a priest.

In our family, we call our prayer corner a home shrine. It is dedicated to Our Lady and has been a center of our family prayer life from the beginning. It is most definitely the center of our family life and often more so! When the kids were little, we taught them to give everything to our Blessed Mother and to go to her in every need. It seems we did our job too well. Not only did special

THE DOMESTIC CHURCH

"Christ chose to be born and grow up in the bosom of the holy family of Joseph and Mary. The Church is nothing other than 'the family of God.' From the beginning, the core of the Church was often constituted by those who had become believers 'together with all [their] household.' ... In our own time, in a world often alien and even hostile to faith, believing families are of primary importance as centers of living, radiant faith. For this reason, the Second Vatican Council, using an ancient expression, calls the family the *Ecclesia domestica*.... It is here that the father of the family, the mother, children, and all members of the family exercise the priesthood of the baptized in a privileged way 'by the reception of the sacraments, prayer and thanksgiving, the witness of a holy life, and self-denial and active charity.' Thus the home is the first school of Christian life and 'school for human enrichment.' Here one learns endurance and the joy of work, fraternal love, generous — even repeated — forgiveness, and above all divine worship in prayer and the offering of one's life."

— Catechism of the Catholic Church (1655-1657)

projects, report cards, and pieces of artwork find their way on to the altar, but also every interesting rock, dead bug, or prize bird feather made its way there too. Sometimes I'd be so embarrassed when people came over and saw all of these strange objects lying there. It looked more like a table at a science fair than an altar! We didn't really care, although I'd have to clean it off periodically so nothing rotted and we'd at least have room for the holy water bottle.

All of us, adults and children, need physical, tangible ways to relate to bigger concepts, especially Divine ones. Being able to place anything they wanted on our altar helped our children develop the confidence that our Blessed Mother was there for them at all times and for all reasons. It opened their hearts to a real mother-child relationship with her.

I made a set of "altar cloths" for our home shrine by hemming the edges of fabric-store remnants. I change them according to the liturgical season: green for Ordinary Time, purple for Lent and Advent, red for Christmas and Pentecost, and a blue one for special feast days of our Blessed Mother. We try to give her fresh flowers, too, whenever possible. During Advent, we set out a miniature wooden crib and gradually fill it with tiny pieces of cotton: one for each sacrifice, extra prayer, or good deed we've done for the baby Jesus in preparation for Christmas. On Christmas Eve, we place a little doll in the crib to represent our newborn King. During Lent, we have a "crown of thorns" made out of twisted construction paper and toothpicks that Matt made years ago. For each offering we do, we put a paper rose petal on one of the toothpick thorns to make it less painful for our dear Lord's precious head. After the Easter Vigil, the crown of thorns is replaced with an Easter lily or other symbol. All of these simple traditions help us to grow in our prayer life and to feel more connected with the universal Church.

We don't need an actual altar — or even an actual prayer corner — to follow Church tradition in our homes. Church traditions can be integrated into the things we already do together as family. For example, the center of the dining room table is a great place for an Advent wreath or crib! It's the same for symbols from other liturgical celebrations, like the crown of thorns. Maybe there's space on the buffet, bookshelf, or entertainment center that can be cleared. We know one family who converted their living room mantle into a prayer corner and another who used the top of a dresser in the parents' bedroom. The particular place isn't the priority; the priority is giving God space in our home and, subsequently, in our hearts.

We also can follow the liturgical seasons through special devotions. There are many beautiful versions of the Stations of the Cross; there also are books of brief, daily Advent reflections, novenas, or Rosary meditations. During the nine days before Christmas, we pray the "shelter seeking novena," which traces the Holy Family's journey to Bethlehem. We also pray a novena to the Holy Spirit on the nine days before Pentecost. Spiritual exercises and devotions that anticipate a liturgical feast day are exceptionally effective in leading the children to a better understanding of its meaning and importance.

Scripture reading is a great way to nourish our faith and increase our knowledge of the Word of God. There's a variety of ways to approach Scripture reading. It might be easiest to begin with the readings for Sunday Mass, which can be found in a Sunday missal or online at a credible Catholic site such as the United States Conference of Catholic Bishops website (www.usccb.org). It's most fruitful if we can read them on Saturday night so the words have time to sink in before Sunday Mass, but even reading them in the car on the way would be helpful. Once we've managed the Sunday readings, we might want to work into the daily Mass readings, available through the same sources.

Lectio divina, or "divine reading," is another way to explore the Word of God, but may be a bit difficult to do as a family, especially those with small children. In its original form, *lectio divina* has four steps: reading, meditation, contemplation, and prayer. Choose a Scripture passage — randomly or from the day's Mass readings — reflect on its meaning, connect it to daily life, and dialogue with God about what's been read and learned. As a family, we might want to have one of the children choose a passage, read it aloud, and then take a little time to discuss it. We could try to picture the scene described in the reading by asking questions like, "Who was there?", "What were they doing?", or "What kind of expression did they have on their faces?" Then we could ask more thoughtful questions like, "What do you think Jesus meant by what he said?", "How does that make you feel?", or "How could we apply that to our own life?" Or we might just want to sit as family, take in the reading, and say nothing at all

All of the things we've been talking about — sacramentals, prayer, Church traditions, and so on — boil down to one thing: striving for holiness. What is holiness, really? It's the result of living in the peace and joy of the beatitudes. The Eight Beatitudes are the heart of Jesus' preaching. We can find them in the Gospel of Matthew, chapter 5, verses 3-11:

> Blessed are the poor in spirit, for theirs is the kingdom of heaven.
>
> Blessed are those who mourn, for they shall be comforted.
>
> Blessed are the meek, for they shall inherit the earth.
>
> Blessed are those who hunger and thirst for righteousness, for they shall be satisfied.
>
> Blessed are the merciful, for they shall obtain mercy.

Blessed are the pure in heart, for they shall see God.

Blessed are the peacemakers, for they shall be called sons of God.

Blessed are those who are persecuted for righteousness' sake, for theirs is the kingdom of heaven.

Blessed are you when men revile you and persecute you and utter all kinds of evil against you falsely on my account. Rejoice and be glad, for your reward is great in heaven.

Christian families are called to live the beatitudes in *and* outside of the home. When Jesus said "feed the hungry" (see Mt 25:35-40), he was asking us to help provide for his people, according to our state of life, means, and abilities. We are all called to apostleship in Christ and obligated to discover how we should carry out our apostolate.

The apostolate can be lived in many ways — anything from bringing meals to an elderly neighbor to working on a political campaign. What we do is less important than how we do it.

When we help others to become holy, we find that we are becoming holier ourselves. There are two things we can guarantee about holiness. First, we are all called to it. Second, we are all able to attain it — sometimes with measurable sweat and tears — through the grace of God. Formerly, people had the notion that only clergy and religious could reach holiness; that couldn't be further from the truth.

Here's what the Church has to say about it in the Second Vatican Council's Dogmatic Constitution on the Church, *Lumen Gentium* (41):

"Furthermore, married couples and Christian parents should follow their own proper path (to holiness) by faithful love. They should sustain one another in grace throughout the entire length of their lives. They should imbue their offspring, lovingly welcomed as God's gift, with Christian doctrine and the evangelical virtues. In this manner, they offer all men the example of unwearying and generous love."

A note of encouragement to single parents: Marriage can in itself be a path to holiness, but it's not a prerequisite for holiness and does not exclude single parents from sanctity. There are plenty of good, holy single parents! We know one Catholic dad who raised his two boys single-handedly. When the boys were small, his wife decided that she was no longer happy in the marriage and wanted out, so he let her go and granted her a divorce. Using his own Catholic faith as a foundation and making use of whatever resources were available to him from the Church, family, and friends, he raised his sons in a markedly Catholic home. Today they are upright young men on their way to doing great things in life.

It's not hard to imagine the Holy Family living the beatitudes. Certainly prayer dominated their daily lives. Where did Joseph and Mary find the twelve-year-old Jesus? He was in the Temple! And our Blessed Mother? Scripture says, "But Mary kept all these things, pondering them in her heart" (Lk 2:19). We can assume that St. Joseph prayed as he worked, since he was a just man and gave to God what is God's. If we want to be like them, we, too, must become families of the beatitudes and prayer.

Married or single, we have many duties in life and many distractions that can deter our own spiritual growth and our children's spiritual growth. We cultivate real sanctity when we allow ourselves to be moved by the Holy Spirit, obey the voice of the heavenly Father, and worship him in spirit and in truth. The Church tells us that each one of us must walk without hesitation — according to our state of life and using the gifts God has given us — on a path of a living faith that awakens hope and charity.

Strength for Your Spirit

"Today our society, more than ever before, needs to know the words of the Gospel and to let itself be transformed by them. Jesus must be able to repeat once again: do not become angry with your neighbors; forgive, and you will be forgiven; tell the truth, to the point of having no need to take an oath; love your enemies; recognize that we have only one Father and are all brothers and sisters; do to others as you would have them do to you. This is the sense of some of the many words from the Sermon on the Mount. If they were lived out, it would be enough to change the world."

— *Chiara Lubich, founder of the Focolare Movement*

Strength for Your Family

1. Do you have a place for prayer set aside in your home? How do you use it? How can you make it come more alive for yourselves and your children?
2. If you don't have a prayer corner, how can you erect one?
3. Do you pray for one another regularly? If not, how can you start? What is a practical means by which you can be reminded to pray for each other?

4. Is Scripture reading a part of your lives? If not, how can you incorporate it into your daily or weekly routine?

5. What is your family apostolate? If you don't have one, how can you become involved in one? Or, how can you develop an apostolic spirit within your home if you're not able to participate outside your home?

Strength for Your Soul

A Prayer for God's Will

Dearest Lord,
teach me to be generous;
teach me to serve you as you deserve;
to give and not to count the cost,
to fight and not to heed the wounds,
to toil and not to seek for rest,
to labor and not to ask for reward
save that of knowing I am doing your will.
Amen.

— St. Ignatius Loyola

Chapter Ten

IN THE BEGINNING

When we build a church, we begin with a physical foundation; when we build a domestic church, we begin with a sacramental foundation. The domestic church is built on the Sacrament of Matrimony. Sadly, the idea of marriage and family is changing.

A November 2010 study by the Pew Research Center shows that 39 percent of Americans believe that marriage is becoming obsolete. Around 34 percent of Americans consider the growing variety of family living arrangements such as unmarried parents and same-sex couples is good for society, while 32 percent said it didn't make a difference, and 29 percent said it was troubling. It's bad enough to have people struggling to keep the institution of marriage from crumbling when the forces of the times and culture threaten to destroy it, but when we tamper with marriage, we tamper with the family. And if we tamper with the family, we tamper with mankind's most basic building block. The Church calls the family the "original cell of social life."

Of course, things happen in spite of our best efforts. Marriages break up, circumstances change, and negative influences affect our families. Regardless, we can never allow our view of marriage, or our belief in it, to be altered. Marriage is a sacrament instituted by Christ and advocated by the Catholic Church. We don't need a Scripture scholar to show us the significance of Jesus' first documented miracle. He highlighted the importance of marriage by miraculously changing the water into wine during the wedding at Cana (see Jn 2:1-11). If Jesus believes so strongly in marriage, then we should, too.

So, what do we know, *really* know, about marriage? The Church is a veritable wellspring of knowledge, inspiration, and direction for married couples. It teaches us that God himself is the author of marriage, that marriage is a vocation (not a mere decision), and that it's a covenant (not a contract) between one man and one woman, with the intention of the procreation and education of children. This indicates that we were created for one another and called by God, not our own human will. We can find this most beautifully described in Scripture: "So they are no longer two, but one. What therefore God has joined together, let no man put asunder" (Mt 19:6).

With this indissoluble covenant, as husband and wife we offer each other mutual support through a bond of selfless, sacrificing love, and we calm our sensuality through intimate, tender love. Marriage makes specific the sanctifying grace of baptism and therefore is a means of sanctification for the couple and the family. As baptized persons, we are members of Christ's body. If I'm a member of Christ's body and my spouse is a member of Christ's body, then I can see Christ in the other. If I can see Christ in the other, I can serve Christ in the other. Finally, if I can see and serve Christ in the other, then the Christ in me will love the Christ in the other. This is true, lasting, mutual love.

With this perspective, "one flesh" — as some translations use for the verse from Matthew — comes to mean so much more than sexual union. It means the union of minds, souls, and spirits. It means that we become one in our daily living and striving. It means we move as one person toward the same aesthetic and spiritual goals. It means that we live in, with, and for one another, always doing first what is best for the other, because that is what is best for ourselves. It means that we do all that is possible to nurture true holiness in the other and through the other, ourselves.

When Mark and I were engaged, the marriage preparation program in our diocese was called "Pre-Cana." It included an interview with a more "experienced" couple who administered our premarital inventory — a lengthy questionnaire asking our individual responses to a variety of situations and opinions on various topics having to do with marriage and family life. We met with the couple a week later to discuss our inventory scores. They were very quiet and kept giving each other awkward glances. Finally, the husband spoke up.

"Mark and Margaret," he said. "We can tell that you two really want to be married. And that's good. But, we're deeply concerned about your inventory scores."

"What do you mean?" Mark asked, pensively.

"Well," the wife tiptoed. 'They're ... uh ... they're so ... uh ... different."

"Different?" I asked.

"Yes," the husband explained. "Your answers are almost completely opposite on a majority of the questions. It's obvious you two don't think alike at all."

"Yes," the wife chimed in, with a bit more courage now. "We worry that your differences could cause problems later."

"But we're not worried about them," I offered. "We've discussed these things, and we know where we each stand."

"Well," the husband said. "We'd like to talk to Father about this first."

They did talk to Father, and Father felt the same way. In fact, he tried to talk us out of getting married. We persisted, and so he gave in. Mark and I knew that even though we held very different opinions on a number of things, we held the exact same opinion on the most important thing: the power of the Sacrament of Matrimony. We knew that if we entered the sacrament with open hearts, God would fill our hearts with the graces that we needed to form a solid, holy marriage. Nearly three decades and four kids later, we not only believe in the power of the sacrament, but we are living proof of that power.

One thing we didn't try to do is change each other after we were married. God created us as unique human beings, and we should accept one another as we are. It's both harmful and immoral to enter into marriage with the presumption that we will change the other to suit ourselves. Have you ever had a boss who expected you to be someone you're not or required you to do tasks that were beyond your capabilities? It's a miserable, stressful situation. When that happens in marriage, it's much worse. If we don't love the person "as is," we have no business marrying him or her.

On the other hand, we can resolve to change ourselves for the sake of our spouse, and that's possible through the activity of God's grace in the sacrament. The Holy Spirit can work miracles. When Mark and I got married, we promised to change for the other. We're not talking about a complete personality makeover here; rather we're talking about changing the things that are within our ability to change. We didn't give the other power to command us to be this way or that way, and we didn't obligate ourselves to jump for the other's every whim. In fact, it's been an extremely rare occurrence that either of us has asked the other to change something. Instead, we sense the other's frustration, hurt, or disappointment and take it upon ourselves to work on the fault or habit that causes the difficulty.

Of course, as imperfect human beings, we can be a little dense, and we don't always pick up on the signals the other is sending out. Take something as simple as coffee. I like my coffee strong. Growing up, we made our coffee in a stovetop percolator and usually forgot about it until it was nearly black as tar and almost as thick. In Mark's family, much more care was taken, and they had "normal" coffee. Once we were married, I made the coffee according to the way it tasted right to me. It was far too strong for Mark, and so he would add water to his coffee in order to lessen its strength. It took me years to actually notice that he was doing this. Once I did notice, I changed my coffee-making methods and attempted to make it weaker. Sometimes it worked; sometimes it didn't. Rather than continue this trial-and-error method of making coffee, Mark suggested that I simply make it the way it seems right to me and he would just add water on the days it turned out too strong. On the days it turned out too weak, I would simply add a few granules of instant coffee. With this, we've both been happy.

Strength for Your Spirit

"The intimate community of life and love which constitutes the married state has been established by the Creator and endowed by him with its own proper laws.... God himself is the 'author of marriage.' The vocation to marriage is written in the very nature of man and woman as they came from the hand of the Creator. Marriage is not a purely human institution despite the many variations it may have undergone through the centuries in different cultures, social structures, and spiritual attitudes. These differences should not cause us to forget its common and permanent characteristics. Although the dignity of this institution is not transparent everywhere with the same clarity, some sense of the greatness of the matrimonial union exists in all cultures. 'The well-being of the individual person and of both human and Christian society is closely bound up with the healthy state of conjugal and family life.'"

— Catechism of the Catholic Church *(1603)*

Strength for Your Family

1. What do you really know about marriage? How can you learn more?

2. How do you promote the sanctity of marriage? To others? To your children?
3. What concepts do you have about changing for the other? Are you willing to do so?

Strength for Your Soul

Prayer of Spouses for Each Other

Lord Jesus, grant that I and my spouse may have a true and understanding love for each other. Grant that we may both be filled with faith and trust. Give us the grace to live with each other in peace and harmony. May we always bear with one another's weaknesses and grow from each other's strengths. Help us to forgive one another's failings and grant us patience, kindness, cheerfulness, and the spirit of placing the well-being of one another ahead of self.

May the love that brought us together grow and mature with each passing year. Bring us both ever closer to you through our love for each other. Let our love grow to perfection.

Amen.

Chapter Eleven

WHO'S IN CHARGE?

Marriage is about changing because we *want* to, not because we *have* to. Our love for one another drives us to improve ourselves and the way we do things for the happiness and comfort of the other and the overall well-being of our marriage. As married persons, we form an intimate community of love and life, an image of the Holy Trinity. I've heard the Trinity described in this way: The Holy Spirit is the love between the Father and the Son. As a married couple, we are like the Trinity in that Christ is the love between husband and wife.

Marriage also is described as a mirror of Christ's love for his Church. St. Paul explains this in his Letters to the Ephesians and Colossians, "Husbands, love your wives, just as Christ loved the church and gave himself up for her…. This is a great mystery, and I mean in reference to Christ and the church; however, let each one of you love his wife as himself, and let the wife see that she respects her husband" (Eph 5:25, 32-33).

Some Bible translations urge wives to obey or be submissive to their husbands, and many a pastor has avoided preaching on that reading in order to avoid the expected flak. That's because we misunderstand it. If we don't listen to these words with open minds and hearts, we can easily take them the wrong way.

St. Paul isn't talking about female enslavement; he's talking about the very essence of the sacrament of marriage: Christ's love. The Church always has and always will teach that men and women are equal in dignity but different in roles, responsibilities, aptitudes, and inclinations. God didn't accidentally create two genders; he willed it so according to his divine plan. God created men and women to be different on purpose.

When St. Paul recommends that wives submit to their husbands, he's comparing Christ's love for the Church with a husband's love for his wife, and vice versa. Everything Jesus did, he did for the benefit of the Church, including dying on the cross. Everything a good husband does, he does for his wife's benefit. A truly godly husband does all in his power to protect, provide for, and respect his wife. He can't order her around, nor can she order him around. Any decisions he makes, he makes in unison with her. He seeks the guidance of the Holy Spirit in all that he does as head of the household.

A wife submits to her husband, not by groveling before him, but by supporting him in his work and responsibilities. St. Paul says that wives should submit to their husbands as to the Lord. Those last four words "as to the Lord" are absolutely key to understanding this concept. How do we submit to the Lord? We love, honor, and respect the Lord because we know that everything he does he does for love of us. A wife loves, honors, and respects her husband because she knows that everything he does he does for love of her. The wife has a great responsibility to help lead her husband toward God, and in that way both the husband and wife are leaders in the relationship.

This requires not a one-sided dictatorship, but rather a royal court in which mutual love, respect, obedience, honor, and trust reign supreme.

One of my pet peeves is wives who gossip about their own husbands. Gossip is dangerous in any form, but it's even worse when it's about our spouses.

One day I was at the hair salon. The stylist and I hit it off really well and talked about all kinds of things. Then the conversation turned toward her husband, and she began complaining about him and disclosing far more information than I should know. At first, I didn't say anything, but she went from mere complaining to outright criticism and, at times, sarcasm. That was enough for me, and I broke into her monologue.

"You know," I said, "any time I have a problem with something my husband does, I go directly to him, because it's nobody else's business."

Her eyebrows shot up and her jaw dropped open. "You wanted the bangs a little shorter this time?" she asked.

That wasn't the first time I've witnessed wives ragging on their husbands behind their backs. I have no doubt that there are husbands who do the same against their wives. Some may call it venting; I call it humiliating our spouses and rotting the cores of our marriages. When we habitually speak negatively about our husbands and wives, we can begin to believe what we say and become resentful. How can we talk that way about the person whom we've promised to cherish above all others? Wives, submit to your husband's right to your respect and trust. Husbands, defend your wife's sensitivity and reputation to the utmost. This is what is meant by marriage as a reflection of Christ's love for his Church.

Where do we more fully experience Christ's love for his Church than in holy Mass? The Eucharist is the "source and summit of the Christian life" (Dogmatic Constitution on the Church, *Lumen Gentium*, 11), and rightfully so. The Eucharist is a memorial of Christ's passion and a sacrifice. The Council of Trent declared that the sacrifice of Christ and the sacrifice of the Eucharist are one single sacrifice. In both sacrifices, the victim is the same (Christ) and only the manner is different. Christ offered himself on the cross, the priest offers Christ in Holy Mass. Thus the sacrifice of the Mass is truly propitiatory. (Propitiation is prayer appealing for the mercy of God on us sinners and for mitigation of punishment justly incurred.)

The Eucharist also is the sacrifice of the Church. We are members of the Mystical Body of Christ, and with him, we offer ourselves whole and entire, uniting ourselves in Christ's intercession with the Father for all of humanity. Our lives — our praise, sufferings, prayer, and work — are united with Christ on the altar and in this way take on new value. Thus all Christians of all generations are united in Christ's offering.

Holy Mass illustrates and gives form to the structure of marriage. Through the Mass, we are united with Christ in a union of life, love, attitude, mission, and sacrifice. We unite in Christ's life of grace, and in his love for the heavenly Father. We join in his attitude of holy subservience, bowing to God's will in all things. We take on his mission to sanctify the world (beginning with ourselves and our family). During Mass, we offer ourselves with Christ to the heavenly Father. We do the same in marriage, surrendering ourselves completely to God and to each other. At Mass we receive renewed strength in Christ and thereby renewed strength to re-espouse ourselves with new fervor. The graces we receive in holy Mass give us the ability to remain true to our marriage vows.

The orientation of holy Mass illustrates the orientation of the marriage covenant. The Mass is offered by the priest as representative of Christ to the heavenly Father. The Father is always at the center. The most important part of the Mass — the Eucharistic Prayer — begins with the preface and closes with a doxology: "Through him, with him, and in him, in unity with the Holy Spirit, all glory and honor is yours, almighty Father, forever and ever. Amen." All is offered with Christ, to the Father, through the hands of the priest. In marriage, all is offered with Christ, to the Father, through our own hands. Just as in Mass, everything in our daily lives is drawn up into God. Just as Christ did, we lovingly, humbly, and obediently place ourselves under the yolk of God's magnificence, giving ourselves completely to him.

This Almighty, All-wise, Unfathomable, and All-kind Father to whom we offer ourselves deserves honor and glory. We offer it to him at Mass, and therefore we also should offer him honor and glory through our marriage. In the Sacrament of Matrimony, we undertake a common path through life that is meant to be a common path to heaven. We work for the sanctification of each other; that which the individual person is less able to do on his or her own should be more attainable through marriage. If it ever were the case that someone could say that after marriage he or she was less directed toward God than before, it would be the death knell of the marriage ideal. Also, we work for our own self-sanctification for the sake of the other. By our being and action, we hope to lead the other closer to God. Through this mutual sanctification we give the Father the honor and glory he deserves.

When we enter the church, we genuflect in reverence before the tabernacle because we know Christ is present within it. Christ in the Eucharist is a great gift to us; the means for our salvation. Our spouse, too, is a great gift to us, and also — although not ontologically the same — the means for our salvation. We should treat our spouse as reverently as we treat Our Lord. Real love begins with deep reverence; love that lacks reverence destroys.

THE DIGNITY OF MARRIAGE

"Christ our Lord has abundantly blessed this love, which is rich in its various features, coming as it does from the spring of divine love and modeled on Christ's own union with the church. Just as of old God encountered his people in a covenant of love and fidelity, so our Savior, the spouse of the Church, now encounters Christian spouses through the sacrament of marriage. He abides with them in order that by their mutual self-giving spouses will love each other with enduring fidelity, as he loved the church and delivered himself for it. Authentic married love is caught up into divine love and is directed and enriched by the redemptive power of Christ and the salvific action of the church, with the result that the spouses are effectively led to God and are helped and strengthened in their lofty role as fathers and mothers. Spouses, therefore, are fortified and, as it were, consecrated for the duties and dignity of their state by a special sacrament; fulfilling their conjugal and family role by virtue of this sacrament, spouses are penetrated with the spirit of Christ and their whole life is suffused by faith, hope and charity; thus they increasingly further their own perfection and their mutual sanctification, and together they render glory to God."

— *"Pastoral Constitution on the Church in the Modern World"* (Gaudium et Spes)

It's not easy to be a truly holy couple. We may become disappointed in our spouse or in ourselves; our human frailty and the effects of original sin make that almost inevitable. Be assured that we'll be sent crosses to carry and trials to endure. That's an inescapable part of married life. What makes the difference is how we approach each difficulty; we can let it either strengthen us or tear us apart.

I was recently visiting with a friend of mine who has survived breast cancer. Since we both tend to be chatterboxes and enjoy each other's company, we talked until it was starting to get late into the evening. As we were talking, my friend's husband came outside with a bottle of water and a couple of pills.

"What have you got there?" she asked.

"It's your sleeping meds," he replied.

"Oh, my goodness! Is it that late?" she exclaimed.

He just smiled and handed her the tablets. She thanked him, took the medication, and handed the bottle back to him. He disappeared back into the house and let us continue our visit.

"Ever since I had the chemotherapy," she explained, almost a little embarrassed at her husband's attentiveness, "I've had insomnia. If I don't take something for it, I'll end up walking the floors all night long."

That little act of kindness so touched me that I thought about it for a good long time afterward. It was more than the husband bringing medication out to his wife, although that in and of itself was most beautiful. It was the fact that even though she was outside (out of sight, out of mind), he remembered the medication on his own and saw to it that his wife took it at the right time so that she could get a good night of sleep. It wasn't his own fatigue he was concerned about; it was hers.

Don't you think that the relationship between our Blessed Mother and St. Joseph was like that? When St.

Joseph discovered that Mary was pregnant, he could have publicly decried her infidelity. He could have solicited the sympathy of relatives and friends. He could have thought only about himself and how painful the situation was for him. Instead, he put Mary first, doing all that he could to preserve her reputation, save her from the possibility of being stoned, and let her go freely. He put Mary's needs before his own, even in such a grave situation!

This gives us a lot to think about as spouses. Are we ready to put the needs of our spouses before our own, even in a grave situation? Can we swallow our pride and preserve the reputation of the other? Perhaps we think we'd never be able to do that. But, by the grace of God, we can. The Church guarantees that the Sacrament of Matrimony gives us the graces we need to live fully our marriage vocation. The sacrament will not fail us even in the toughest of times if we faithfully call upon its resources and look to the Church for help and guidance. These words quoted by Blessed John Paul II during his General Audience on August 3, 1994, should continuously echo in our hearts:

> As the Second Vatican Council said, Christian married couples "should imbue their offspring, lovingly welcomed as God's gift, with Christian doctrine and the evangelical virtues" (*Lumen Gentium*, 41). It is the most essential apostolate of family life. This work of giving their children moral and spiritual formation also sanctifies the parents, who are themselves blessed with a deeper, renewed faith, as the experience of Christian families often shows.

Marriage is a noble, vital, sacred institution, and we must not let anyone try to convince us it's not. Anything we can do — large or small — to testify to that fact is worth the effort. In our work for the Schoenstatt Movement, Mark and I do a lot of e-mailing, particularly with married couples. In every salutation or greeting, we purposefully include the names of both the husband and wife, even if we're responding to an e-mail sent by only one of the spouses. Mark and I address both members of the couple for symbolic reasons. It's one small but important way to acknowledge the sanctity of marriage, declaring its necessity for the posterity of society, and witnessing to its beauty.

Strength for Your Spirit

> "Marriage is a sacrament that makes one flesh of two bodies. Theology expresses this fact in a striking way when it teaches us that the matter of the sacrament is the bodies of husband and wife. Our Lord sanctifies and blesses the mutual love of husband and wife. He foresees, not only a union of souls, but a union of bodies as well. No Christian, whether or not he is called to the married state, has a right to underestimate the value of marriage."

— *Blessed Josemaria Escriva, Founder of Opus Dei*

Strength for Your Family

1. Discuss St. Paul's passages about marriage in Ephesians 5:25 and Colossians 3:19. What do those passages mean to you?
2. What does "equal in dignity but different in roles" look like, in practical terms, in your family?
3. Do you defend and protect each other's reputation? How?

4. Do you attend daily Mass? How can you make it a more fulfilling experience for your marriage? If you don't go, could you start, even if it's once or twice a week?
5. Do you show reverence for each other? How?

Strength for Your Soul

Prayer of St. Bonaventure to the Holy Spirit

Lord Jesus, as God's Spirit came down and rested upon you,
May the same Spirit rest on us,
Bestowing his sevenfold gifts.
First, grant us the gift of understanding,
By which your precepts may enlighten our minds.
Second, grant us counsel, by which we may follow
in your footsteps on the path of righteousness.
Third, grant us courage,
by which we may ward off the enemy's attacks.
Fourth, grant us knowledge,
by which we can distinguish good from evil.
Fifth, grant us piety,
by which we may acquire compassionate hearts.
Sixth, grant us fear,
by which we may draw back from evil
and submit to what is good.
Seventh, grant us wisdom,
that we may taste fully the life-giving sweetness of your love.
Amen.

Chapter Twelve

UNITED WE STAND

I love it when our older kids drop in for an impromptu visit. It's so much fun to hear about what they've been up to, what's going on in their lives, and what they think about what's going on in the world. The kids know that Dad's always up for a debate, especially since I refuse to debate him. It's useless; I will lose every time. Sometimes, when the mood and setting are right, the kids will seek me out for a heart-to-heart about less public things that are on their minds like school, friends, love interests, pending decisions, or religion.

Mark and I feel privileged. We know parents whose kids won't give them the time of day, much less a whole conversation. We even have friends who swear they'll be the last to know even the most important things about their kids, like wedding dates and the birth of their first grandchildren. The kids definitely have things they don't feel comfortable talking about with us, and that's okay. They have a right to their privacy. But, for the most part, we have a very open relationship.

On one of Monica's visits, she wandered into the kitchen while I was making supper. Mark was there, too, as we'd been chatting. She asked some inconsequential questions and then said, "I just want to thank you two for never having fought in front of us kids."

We were stunned. "What brought this on?" I asked, puzzled.

"I know so many people who talk about how their parents fight all the time," she said. "Like this one friend whose parents never stop fighting and it just tears her apart. She can't stand it!"

"But," I said, "it's not like your dad and I never disagreed."

"That's exactly it," she went on. "You disagreed, but you never fought in front of us. Oh, sure, there were times we could sense you weren't exactly happy with each other and things were a little tense. But then, somehow, it just disappeared, and things were okay again. Thank you! Thank you so much! You have no idea what a great thing that's been for us kids."

It's true we made a concerted effort never to disagree in front of the kids. You can be sure there were times when we were ready to kill each other (figuratively speaking), but we always settled it in private.

Mark and I joke that we learned what *to* do from his parents and what *not* to do from mine. In spite of their best efforts, my parents sometimes broke into fights in front of us kids. As a very sensitive child, this scared the daylights out of me. I'd run and hide someplace until it was all over. Mark remembers one single fight between his parents. One! They verbally tussled over the right of a person to ruin a good steak with ketchup, and then it was over and all was well. The rest of the time the kids never suspected when their parents had a disagreement. Mom Fenelon still chuckles over "the" fight. That's truly remarkable. So, between the two sets of parents, we figured out that it's not a good idea to fight in front of the kids.

There are other reasons not to fight. Kids who witness their parents' marital conflict don't easily forget them. Consider how, well into adulthood, Monica's friend was feeling the effects of her parents' fighting. According to Catholic family therapist Thomas Schmierer, emotionally-charged situations trigger our innate survival mechanism, and our senses become "hyper-tuned." We take in more information, and it becomes imprinted in our brains. For example, most of us can remember exactly what we were doing on 9/11 because it was such a traumatic event. Parental conflicts are like mini-terrorist attacks for our children.

How we handle conflict affects the emotional security and future emotional adjustment and behavior of our children. Two 2006 studies conducted by researchers from the University of Notre Dame, University of Rochester, and the Catholic University of America, and published in the January/February 2006 issue of the journal *Child Development* provide powerful evidence for this.

In the first study, 226 parents and their nine- to eighteen-year-old children were monitored over a period of three years. Researchers examined the connection between marital conflict and emotional problems and found that destructive marital conflict such as personal insults, defensiveness, withdrawal, sadness, or fear started a snowball effect that later resulted in emotional insecurity and maladjustment in the children, including depression, anxiety, and behavior problems, even when researchers controlled for any initial adjustment problems.

In the second study, a different group of 232 parents and kindergarten-age children were monitored over three years. Researchers again found that marital conflict prompt events that led to later emotional insecurity and maladjustment in the children, even when they controlled for any initial emotional problems. Both studies considered everyday types and sources of conflict such as arguments over child-care and household responsibilities.

PEACE BEGINS IN THE FAMILY

"In a healthy family life we experience some of the fundamental elements of peace: justice and love between brothers and sisters, the role of authority expressed by parents, loving concern for the members who are weaker because of youth, sickness or old age, mutual help in the necessities of life, readiness to accept others and, if necessary, to forgive them. For this reason, the family is the first and indispensable teacher of peace."

— *Pope Benedict XVI, World Day of Peace, January 1, 2008*

Since the studies involved representative community samples, the researchers feel certain that the findings can be generalized to most American families.

When our kids were little, a familiar scenario played itself out time and again in the Fenelon Clan abode. I'd be busy with writing or household chores and would suddenly hear heated voices in the other room. Then I'd hear more below-the-breath rumblings, some scuffling, and a thump or two.

"What's going on in there?" I'd shout.

"Uh, nothing!" one would answer.

"That's not true!" the other would accuse. "He … "

The second child's words drowned out by the first, "We lo-o-o-v-e-e you, Mom!"

Well, then I *knew* something serious was up, so I'd set down whatever I was working on and go check it out. The second I entered the room, I'd be bombarded with tales of accusations, injustices, offenses, and threats. The worst part was that none of them made sense to me, and it was impossible to tell who was really at fault. It was frustrating, to say the least.

That's how it is for kids when parents fight, but a hundredfold more stressful. Kids don't usually have the maturity to deal with their own conflict, much less their parents'. When their parents fight, they can feel caught in the middle, trying to figure out who is at fault and how to achieve resolution. What's more, they can't always tell the severity of the situation; what could be a minor disagreement to the parents could feel like the end of the marriage — and along with it, the end of the world — to the children. That can leave them feeling confused and helpless.

Things can be made much worse when name-calling and insults are involved. In our house, both of them are absolutely taboo for parents and children alike.

It's more than a matter of flying words. When we name-call or insult another human being, we're violating the Fifth Commandment. Even if we're not murdering the person, even if we're not inflicting any bodily harm at all, names and insults "kill" a little part of the other by marring their dignity as a child of God. We can be angry — anger is a natural emotion — but we may not express it in derogatory terms.

No matter how hard we try, there will be times when conflict erupts, either covertly or overtly. These are excellent times to teach our kids (and ourselves) positive conflict resolution.

The Notre Dame, Rochester, and Catholic University of America researchers also found that constructive marital conflict, especially when parents express physical affection, positive feelings, compromise, or problem solving, actually increases children's security and helps them learn how to handle conflict constructively themselves.

Family therapist Schmierer recommends a double-loop method of resolving conflict. He explains that, typically, couples face conflict in one of two extreme ways. They either avoid the conflict altogether or they debate it. In between those two extremes lies some form of collaboration such as the double loop, in which everyone's needs are seen as important. The model he uses in his practice looks like this:

Person A: verbalizes (1) the behavior of the other person and (2) how this made him feel. This is done non-judgmentally, simply expressing the behavior and the feeling.

Person B: Feeds back to Person A what he understands him to be saying. For example, "So, when I ... you felt ... "

Person B: Checks in with Person A. "Did I understand you, correctly? Did I get that right?"

Person A: If Person A feels understood, the double loop is complete. If Person A doesn't feel understood, then he corrects Person B and starts over from step one. Person A will know immediately if he feels understood because he will experience a sensation of relaxation and release of tension in his body when he knows he is understood. He will instantly feel more connected to his feelings and more connected to Person B.

This method of communication does not resolve disagreements about the *content* of what is being discussed, but it quickly removes roadblocks in the *process* of the communication, which is where the majority of relational difficulties take place.

At first, it can be awkward to put this into practice, but it will feel easier and more natural after it has been used a few times. This pattern of communication and understanding plays a dramatic role in helping Person A become more assertive and expressive, both during and after a marital conflict.

If it's bad to speak against our spouse to other adults, it's devastating to do so to our children. This doesn't mean we have to make it seem as though everything our spouse does is right even when it's not. If there's a truly dangerous or abusive situation, we're obligated to intervene and seek professional help, but those day-to-day things that bother or even infuriate us are better kept to ourselves and discussed privately with our spouse.

Years ago, a friend of mine told me that her twelve-year-old daughter was exceptionally sensitive to any kind of correction given by her husband. Even the mildest comment would elicit a flood of tears. My friend noticed that her husband could seem harsh at times even though he didn't mean to be. Rather than feed into her daughter's unhappiness, she quietly discussed the situation with her husband when they were alone. Once he was made aware of the problem, he changed his approach, and things improved dramatically. Today father and daughter have a close, loving relationship — one that could have been short-circuited if my friend hadn't acted so wisely.

Decision-making also is best done privately between husband and wife, unless it's one that requires input from the whole family. Even then, the decision is up to the couple, not the kids, and ultimately up to Dad, as head of the household.

If you haven't figured it out yet, it doesn't take kids long to learn how to play parents against each other, given the opportunity. How many times has the following happened to us?

"Dad, can I play a video game?" asks perceptive youngster.

"Sure," says unsuspecting Dad. "But watch the time limit."

"You bet! Thanks, Dad!" responds perceptive youngster.

Mom goes into the living room to water the plants and sees perceptive youngster playing the video game.

"Are you all done cleaning your bedroom already?" she says, pleased.

"Uh … no," says perceptive youngster.

"Then why are you playing video games?" annoyed Mom asks.

"Dad said I could," perceptive youngster responds.

We've experienced this countless times. Now, whenever any kid asks either of us for anything, we ask what the other parent has decreed before even venturing a response.

Kids don't mean to be devious — they're simply opportunists. If they learn to play us against each other in the little things, they'll play us against each other in the big things. That's why it's vital for our kids to see parents as one, united authority rather than two separate ones.

Occasionally, we still make the mistake of granting something without checking with the other first. In that case, we use the opportunity to teach humility.

"You know what?" embarrassed Mom says to perceptive youngster. "I made a terrible mistake. I should have checked with Dad first before I gave you permission to go to Jody's house. That was wrong of me. Your dad told you that you weren't allowed to hang out with friends this week because you failed the last math exam. You need more study time. I'm sorry. I'm going to have to take back my permission."

Parents can be opportunists, too.

Strength for Your Spirit

"Finally, let the spouses themselves, made to the image of the living God and enjoying the authentic dignity of persons, be joined to one another in equal affection, harmony of mind and the work of mutual sanctification. Thus, following Christ who is the principle of life, by the sacrifices and joys of their vocation and through their faithful love, married people can become witnesses of the mystery of love which the Lord revealed to the world by his dying and his rising up to life again."

— Pastoral Constitution on the
Church in the Modern World,
Gaudium et Spes, *December 7, 1965*

Strength for Your Family

1. Do you fight in front of the children? When?
2. What safeguards can you put in place to ensure that your conflicts are resolved in private?
3. How do you resolve your conflicts? In what ways can you improve your method?
4. How can you prevent crossing one another's authority and decisions?

Strength for Your Soul

A Marriage Prayer

Merciful Father,

We are together on Earth, alone in the universe.

Look at us and help us to love one another.

Teach us to understand each other, just as you understand us.

Make our souls as fresh as the morning.
Make our hearts as innocent as the Lamb.
May we forgive each other, and forget the past,
and may we have peace inside — and in our world.
Today and forever.
Amen.

— Catholic Family Prayer Book

Chapter Thirteen

THE PRINCIPAL'S OFFICE

The Church has given all parents a huge and most important responsibility: the education of our children. Just as the Church as an entity is both a governing and teaching body, so is the domestic church.

Basically, the Church is telling us to educate our children *together*. However, even though we moms and dads work together as educators of our children, we will not educate them in the same way. Men will educate in a fatherly way, women will educate in a motherly way, and children need to experience both in order to wholly develop. The *Catechism of the Catholic Church* tells us that we complement each other not only sexually, but also as helpmates for man and woman were "made for each other," and "as spouses and parents cooperate in a unique way in the Creator's work" (372).

When a child falls and skins his knee, most often he will run to his mom before he'll run to his dad. That's no offense to his dad; it merely means that he intuitively recognizes his mom as the more nurturing of the two. In general, moms are the ones who do the snuggling, cuddling, appeasing, and pleasing. Just look at the symbolic value of the woman's body. Her primary sexual organs show a strong openness, signaling a strong receptivity, that is, the ability and the need to receive. Her secondary sexual organs symbolize the giving of self. The spiritual character

PARENTS AS PRIMARY EDUCATORS

"Since parents have given children their life, they are bound by the most serious obligation to educate their offspring and therefore must be recognized as the primary and principal educators. This role in education is so important that only with difficulty can it be supplied where it is lacking. Parents are the ones who must create a family atmosphere animated by love and respect for God and man, in which the well-rounded personal and social education of children is fostered. Hence the family is the first school of the social virtues that every society needs. It is particularly in the Christian family, enriched by the grace and office of the Sacrament of Matrimony, that children should be taught from their early years to have a knowledge of God according to the faith received in baptism, to worship Him, and to love their neighbor. Here, too, they find their first experience of a wholesome human society and of the Church. Finally, it is through the family that they are gradually led to a companionship with their fellowmen and with the people of God. Let parents, then, recognize the inestimable importance a truly Christian family has for the life and progress of God's own people."

— *Pope Paul VI, "Declaration on Christian Education,"* Gravis- simum Educationis, *October 28, 1965, 3*

of the soul of a woman is a pronounced receiving and self-giving, therefore forming a strong urge within her to give of herself and receive from others.

Because of her inherent qualities, woman fulfills three main tasks. First, she is the giver and guardian of life. She cares for that life both before and after the birth of the child in a very intimate way, and continues to develop life through service to her family. Second, she develops the intellectual and emotional life. The mother awakens the child to the world around him and is the main socializing influence in his early life. Through the mother, the child learns how to relate to other people, although this is also true of the child's relationship with his father. The mother helps the child to combine ideas and life, and teaches the child love, loyalty, concern, consideration, service, and dedication through her guidance and by embodying these characteristics herself. Third, she tends to be the main religious influence in the home. The mother often takes the lead in creating a religious atmosphere in the home and in providing tangible religious experiences for the family. In general, it's the mother who fosters home customs and initiates religious practices.

Using the Blessed Mother as model, all women, whether single or married, are called to three roles: virgin, mother, and spouse. As virgin, women are called to be open to God and completely filled by his grace. As mother, women are called to give and serve selflessly, to nurture through sacrifice, service, and total love. As spouse, women are called to be helpmate, partner, and companion. There is an old saying that if the heart of the mother is an altar of sacrifice, you may be sure that the home soon will resemble a church.

On the other hand, whenever a child has a yearning to do something adventurous, he generally goes to his dad.

Nearly every summer since the kids were little, we've gone to Mark's brother's cabin on a lake in central

Wisconsin. About two hours from the cabin lies Copper Falls, a scenic state park with gorgeous hiking trails and, of course, waterfalls. Great, high, waterfalls with teeny-weeny little wooden footbridges that go over vast, abyss-like gorges. They're the kind that could swallow a kid up and never spit him back out. It's fine for people who don't mind their life hanging from a thread, but for those of us (me) who prefer our feet on solid footing, it's a nightmare.

The first and only time I ever went, I didn't know what I was in for. We packed a picnic lunch and decided to make a day of it, hiking the trails, and enjoying the scenery. It was a beautiful day. We got to Copper Falls, parked the car, and ate our picnic lunch. Then we gathered our things, and headed for the trails. It was absolutely wonderful! Wonderful, that is, until we reached the first set of falls and I saw that narrow bridge over that enormous open space. I looked at Mark. I looked at the expanse beneath us. I looked at Mark. I look at the bridge. I swallowed hard. I didn't want the kids to sense my fear because I didn't want to teach them to be afraid of "new" experiences. Suddenly, Mom felt very, very, tired. "Well, kids," I said, trying to sound brave. "All this fresh air is making me really sleepy. I think it's better for me to go back to the car and have a little nap while you guys go ahead and enjoy the hike."

"Aw, too bad!" They all said in unison. "Okay, Dad! Let's go!"

And off they went without even giving me another thought. Dad wasn't tired, and he led the way with vim and vigor across the bridge, with the kids excitedly trekking right behind him.

Of course, it's pretty obvious that I don't care for footbridges over gorges. I use this example to demonstrate the difference between moms and dads and how their children see them. It didn't bother the kids one bit that I didn't want to go along; they had pegged Dad as the more daring of the two of us. For the most part, that's how dads are. Even their physique shows this; they have a more extroverted makeup with their primary sexual organs on the outside of their bodies. Men are the conquerors, providers, and protectors. They offer security and strength. Their greatest reward is knowing that their wife and children are well cared for.

Because of this, the father is the fundamental authority of the family. As such, he is called to be a reflection of God the Father for his children. Jesus' words that "You, therefore, must be perfect, as your heavenly Father is perfect" (Mt 5:48) apply to dads in a very special way. Without the experience of a loving father on the human level, children can have an extremely difficult time forming a loving relationship with God the Father when they are adults. The greatest apostolate a man can do as a male and as a father is to show God to his children.

Dads must be good to their kids even if their kids are not good to them, in order to reflect the heavenly Father's goodness and mercy. Consider the prodigal son (see Lk 15:11-32). The son left home with his share of the inheritance, thinking he knew better than his dad. He squandered everything he had, ended up eating the fodder of pigs, and returned home in defeat. What did the father do? He welcomed his son back with arms wide open. This doesn't mean that fathers — or mothers, for that matter — must accept disrespect and misbehavior from their children. It means that the father bears his family in his heart and acts always with the utmost benevolence toward them while guiding his children in godly ways.

Strength for Your Spirit

"Man and woman have been created, which is to say, willed by God: on the one hand, in perfect equality as human persons; on the other, in their respective beings as man and woman. 'Being man' or 'being woman' is a reality which is good and willed by God: man and woman possess an inalienable dignity which comes to them immediately from God their Creator. Man and woman are both with one and the same dignity 'in the image of God.' In their 'being-man' and 'being-woman,' they reflect the Creator's wisdom and goodness."

— Catechism of the Catholic Church (369)

Strength for Your Family

1. In what ways do you demonstrate fatherliness/motherliness to your children?
2. How can you help each other to be more fatherly/motherly?
3. Is the father the fundamental authority in your family? If not, how can you work together to assure that he is, while at the same time maintaining the role of mother as supporting authority?

Strength for Your Soul

Prayer for Mothers

Loving God,

as a mother gives life and nourishment to her children,

so you watch over your Church.

Bless our mother.

Let the example of her faith and love shine forth.
Grant that we, her family,
may honor her always
with a spirit of profound respect.
Grant this through Christ our Lord.
Amen.

Prayer for Fathers

God, you are the giver of all life,
human and divine.
Bless our father.
May he be the best of teachers for his children,
bearing witness to the faith
by what he says and does,
in Christ Jesus our Lord.
Amen.

> *–United States Conference of Catholic Bishops,*
> Catholic Household Blessings & Prayers,
> Revised Edition

Chapter Fourteen

COUNTERING CULTURE

Culturally, the understanding of true fatherhood and true motherhood is dramatically changing, mostly for the worst. For decades, popular media has portrayed the father as kind of a bumbler, somebody who means well but who somehow never manages to do things right. Think of popular television shows like *Everybody Loves Raymond* or *The Simpsons*. They can be humorous and heartwarming at times, but the dad frequently takes the brunt of all the jokes. It wouldn't be so bad if those two were the only shows, but there are many like them.

At the same time, modern culture has diminished the vitality of motherhood. With good reason, the women's rights movement has emancipated women from unjust laws and dehumanization. The problem is that the movement has also "emancipated" them from moral law. The focus of woman has changed from expecting to serve to expecting to be served. Modern society, especially our entertainment industry, portrays women as divas who aren't obligated to anybody but themselves. Just think of the growing number of female celebrities who choose to have a child with or without a spouse simply because they've decided it's something they want at this time in their lives. After childbirth, they get themselves back into shape and return to the stage performing the same often lewd and sexually-charged antics.

These detrimental trends will begin to reverse only when we start working together as man and woman. True fathers help women to be true mothers, and true mothers help men to be true fathers. There's a polar unity between the two, and our children — the entire generation, not just those who reside within our homes — need both motherliness and fatherliness in order to develop into fully-rounded personalities. Motherliness and fatherliness supplement and complement each other. Mothers need the authority of the fathers to support them; fathers need the intuitiveness of the mother to balance their authority.

When our older kids reached the age of reason (that is, became old enough to consciously misbehave), I'd deal with it by threatening, "Wait until your father gets home!" It didn't take me long to realize that if I continued to respond to their naughtiness in this manner, the kids would soon learn to walk all over me. If we were going to survive as a family, I'd have to figure something out quick. I put together a system of discipline that would work for me, including time-outs, removal of privileges, and extra chores. It helped tremendously, if not a bit too much. The kids started to look to me as the primary authority instead of Mark. This just wouldn't do! Dad cannot be relegated to the position of bystander in his own home. So I had to make another adjustment. Since discipline is most effective when rendered immediately, I'd go ahead and render it. If it was something minor, I'd let it go at that and tell Mark about it later. If it were something significant, I'd discipline the child and then call Mark at work to "clue him in." That night, he'd make a little strategic conversation at the supper table.

"So, Matt (or Monica or Luke or John … they all had their turns)," Mark would say, pushing himself slightly back from the table and casually crossing one leg over the other. "How was your day?"

"Fine," Matt (Monica, Luke, John) would respond, staring intently at his or her plate. It's amazing just how fascinating a noodle can be.

"Did anything interesting happen?" Mark would ask calmly.

"No, not really," Matt (Monica, Luke, John) would answer and cringe, barely breathing.

"Not really? Well, tell me about chore time this morning," Mark would continue.

Of course, the child was busted and had no choice but to 'fess up, at which point Mark would either second the discipline I'd levied or add to it, depending on the severity of the infraction. Civil authorities might accuse us of child entrapment. What we really were doing, however, was showing the kids that Mom and Dad are always on the same page, and that Dad's fatherliness backs Mom's motherliness.

What if one parent disagrees with the discipline given by the other? First of all, no displeasure is expressed to the child. Instead, Dad and Mom discuss it in private and reach a mutually agreeable solution. Then, the parent who issued the discipline goes back to the child, informs him that Dad and Mom have reconsidered the situation and *they* think the discipline should be changed to whatever it is that was agreed upon in private. Never, ever, does one parent undermine the authority of the other!

It's not only what we *don't* do in front of our kids that helps them grow into healthy adults; it's also what we *do* do in front of them. As a couple, we want to build a culture of chaste and holy tenderness that forms a community of love in our home beginning with the two of us.

CALLED TO HOLINESS

"God's design for marriage and the family must be striven after responsibly.... [T]he moral law [is not] ... merely an ideal to be achieved in the indefinite future. Pope John Paul II explains that married people must embody the values enshrined in the law of God through concrete actions. 'And so what is known as "the law of gradualness" or step-by-step advance cannot be identified with "gradualness of the law," as if there were different degrees or forms of precept in God's law for different individuals and situations. In God's plan, all husbands and wives are called in marriage to holiness.'"

— Cardinal J. Francis Stafford,
President of the Pontifical Council for the Laity

That includes physical affection. If we as a couple don't demonstrate pure and natural touch to our children, how will they learn to give it to others? If the only time we're touching each other is in the bedroom, we've got a problem. If we're touching each other sexually outside of the bedroom (in view of the children), then we've got an even bigger problem. Kids already are bombarded with sexual gestures, innuendos, and images in the media. If that's all they ever see, that's all they'll ever expect.

It's not only good but also vitally important that our kids see us hugging, giving each other an innocent kiss, holding hands, sitting together, and genuinely enjoying being around each other. It shows them that a male and female can be in a loving relationship without having to constantly hop into bed together. Additionally, it makes them feel more loved and secure. When kids sense that their parents truly, tenderly care for each other, they become more self-assured and better able to form solid friendships and love relationships later in life.

For years, we've invited groups of young adults to our home for a "Souper Supper" — a meal of homemade soup and fresh bread, companionship, and animated conversation. The repeaters know to expect a hug from me upon entering and leaving. I give everybody a warm, motherly hug unless I sense that they're uncomfortable with that. I always get a chuckle out of the newcomers — their responses range from utter shock, to complete confusion, to absolute joy. Some of them give me an awkward pat on the back, but some of them act as if I'm a life preserver, and they hang on for dear life. I suspect many of them never receive pure, chaste affection from anyone and are amazed at how wonderful it can be. If I don't give it to them, they might not get it from anybody else. If I show them how, they may learn to do it for others. If pure chaste touch can do that for visitors, imagine what it can do for our own children.

As educators, parents guide their children in learning how to use both their intellect and intuition. The mind of the man, who thinks, plans, and builds, needs the heart of the woman, who perceives, responds, and shelters. No doubt this is not an absolute; there are men who are incredibly perceptive, and there are women who are great planners. It's the mix of the two and the way they complement each other that matters most. When we work in supplementation and complementation, our children reap immeasurable benefits.

This reminds me of the Holy Family's flight to Egypt. The angel appeared to St. Joseph, not to the Blessed

Mother, telling him to take the child and mother and flee for the sake of their safety (see Mt 2:13-20). By appearing to St. Joseph, the angel acknowledges that he is the authority and protector of the family. And the Blessed Mother's role? Scripture doesn't say specifically, but we can imagine that she was the one to prepare Our Lord for the trip, carefully wrapping him in warm clothing and seeing to his comfort along the way. When it was safe for the Holy Family to return to Israel, the angel again appeared to St. Joseph, not to Mary. In the Holy Family — as it should be in ours — the father was the head and the mother was the heart, uniting to form an inseparable whole.

Strength for Your Spirit

"If the man is the head of the family, the woman is the heart, and as he occupies the chief place in ruling, so she may and ought to claim for herself the chief place love."

— *Pope Pius XI, Encyclical Letter on Marriage,*
Casti Cannubii, *December 31, 1930*

Strength for Your Family

1. How can you, as a family, promote respect for fatherhood and motherhood?
2. As a couple, do you complement each other?
3. Do you demonstrate chaste affection in front of your children and to your children? How can you become better at it?
4. How can you increase the spirit of teamwork within your marriage?

Strength for Your Soul

Prayer for Wisdom

O Light of the World, Infinite God, Father of Eternity, giver of Wisdom and Knowledge, and ineffable dispenser of every Spiritual Grace; who knowest all things before they are made, who makest the darkness and the light; put forth thy hand and touch my mouth, and make it as a sharp sword to utter eloquently thy words.

Make my tongue, O Lord, as a chosen arrow, to declare faithfully thy wonders.

Put thy Spirit, O Lord, in my heart, that I may perceive; in my soul, that I may retain; and in my conscience, that I may meditate.

Do thou lovingly, holily, mercifully, clemently and gently inspire me with thy grace. Do thou teach, guide and strengthen the comings in and goings out of my senses and my thoughts.

And let thy discipline instruct me even to the end, and the Counsel of the Most High help me through thy tnfinite wisdom and mercy. Amen.

— *St. Anthony of Padua*

Chapter Fifteen

ATTITUDE IS EVERYTHING

Anytime a tough situation comes up, our kids automatically know that Mark and I will tell them: "Pay close attention. For as difficult (confusing, painful, stressful … you name it) this situation is, there's a message in it for you from God." It's not a put-off; we really mean it. They probably get ticked off at us every once in a while for saying that, because they're hoping for a quick fix to a problem. Actually, Mark and I wouldn't mind some quick fixes ourselves. But there's seldom a quick fix to anything; only subtle and sometimes not-so-subtle answers that come to us from God over time.

If we want to receive those answers, we need to form an intense attachment to God, one that goes beyond obeying the Ten Commandments to desiring with all our hearts to please him in everything we think, say, and do. We want our attachment to God to be harmonious, so that we're really "in tune" with him, sensing his desires for us according to our state of life, work, and relationship to others. We also want our attachment to be more than a lofty idea; we want it to be something we tangibly practice in our daily lives. Finally, we want our attachment to God to permeate every aspect of our lives. This is the attitude of the saints, and if we want to reach heaven as they did, it must become our attitude, too.

The root of holiness — the attitude of the saints — is a constant awareness of the presence of God. He isn't a nebulous power that hangs around in outer space getting his jollies by manipulating the lives of human beings. He's truly and completely a father, and he's not just *a* father, he's *our* father.

St. Paul often spoke about God's fatherhood:

"For all who are led by the Spirit of God are sons of God. For you did not receive the spirit of slavery to fall back into fear, but you have received the spirit of sonship. When we cry, "Abba! Father" it is the Spirit himself bearing witness with our spirit that we are children of God, and if children, then heirs, heirs of God and fellow heirs with Christ, provided we suffer with him in order that we may also be glorified with him" (Rom 8:14-17).

The spirit of sonship of which St. Paul speaks is also an attitude of childlikeness. The heavenly Father has given us something that no biological or adoptive father can give his child: a share in his own life. We're made in the image and likeness of God and united to him because of his grace. In baptism, our souls received what had been given in paradise, but lost by original sin. We received a new divine life and therefore became truly children of God and began to share in his divine activity of knowledge and love. And so, if God is the King that makes us royal children, we want to act accordingly.

St. Peter tells us:

"May grace and peace be multiplied to you in the knowledge of God and of Jesus our Lord. His divine power has granted to us all things that pertain to life and godliness, through the knowledge of him who called us to his own glory and excellence, by which he has granted to us his precious and very great promises, that through these you may escape from the corruption that is in the world because of passion, and become partakers of the divine nature. For this very reason make every effort to supplement your faith with virtue, and virtue with knowledge, and knowledge with self-control, and self-control with steadfastness, and steadfastness with godliness, and godliness with brotherly affection, and brotherly affection with love" (2 Pt 1:2-7).

The heavenly Father has called us to his own glory and excellence. As royal children, we take on a royal attitude. It's royal in that we hold ourselves accountable to rise above the degradation and godlessness of the world around us. It's royal in that we adhere to a scale of values that uplifts and inspires us. It's royal in that we don't think we're better than others but work to become better than we are. It's royal in that we're granted the ability to know and love God, to walk in the Holy Spirit, and to love whatever God loves. It's royal in that we live in the reality that we are cherished by God above all things.

According to the Church, through our baptism we become not only a royal people, but also priests and prophets. As a royal people, a royal married couple, a royal family, our vocation is to serve — with Christ — each other, our Church, and the world in that order of priority, thus fulfilling our royal dignity. Because we are royalty, we live in the "court" of the King's heart, attaching ourselves to him and aligning ourselves to his will for the sake of the Kingdom.

When England's Prince William announced his engagement to Kate Middleton in November 2010, the pa-

PRIESTLY, PROPHETIC, ROYAL

"Jesus Christ is the one whom the Father anointed with the Holy Spirit and established as priest, prophet, and king. The whole People of God participates in these three offices of Christ and bears the responsibilities for mission and service that flow from them.

"On entering the People of God through faith and Baptism, one receives a share in this people's unique, priestly vocation'. ... The holy People of God shares also in Christ's prophetic office,' above all in the supernatural sense of faith that belongs to the whole People, lay and clergy, when it 'unfailingly adheres to this faith ... once for all delivered to the saints,' and when it deepens its understanding and becomes Christ's witness in the midst of this world.

"Finally, the People of God shares in the royal office of Christ. He exercises his kingship by drawing all men to himself through his death and Resurrection. Christ, King and Lord of the universe, made himself the servant of all, for he came 'not to be served but to serve, and to give his life as a ransom for many.' For the Christian, 'to reign is to serve him,' particularly when serving 'the poor and the suffering, in whom the Church recognizes the image of her poor and suffering founder.'"

— Catechism of the Catholic Church (783-786)

parazzi went wild, and so did the rest of the world. Not only had it been a several-years-long romance, but Prince William gave Ms. Middleton the exquisite sapphire engagement ring that had belonged to his mother, the late

Princess Diana. At the time of Princess Diana's engagement to Prince Charles in 1981, the ring was worth $30,000; current estimates place it in the half-million dollar range. Prince William explained to reporters that the ring was very special to him; giving it to his fiancée was his way of making sure his mother was somehow included in the excitement of the engagement and the ensuing marriage celebration. The ring is important, not only for its value, but also for its history, since it is a symbol of the couple's royal heritage. Ms. Middleton accepted it with great delight and the consciousness of what it symbolizes; after all, the man she married in the spring of 2011 is heir to the throne of England. Its presence on her finger is a constant reminder of her role as the Duchess of Cambridge and her future role as the Queen of England.

We, too, possess a royal jewel, a reminder of our heritage, of who we are, and what's expected of us. But our "ring" is worth a whole lot more than the Duchess' ring — it's worth eternity. It's the grace of God within us; it reminds us that we are royal children of God and that we're expected to be the light and salt of the earth. Our jewel commits us, through baptism, to a perpetual and deepening relationship with the heavenly Father. Like the Duchess' ring, it's a right of entry into the royal family.

Strength for Your Spirit

"And the Word became flesh! … in order to make us earthly beings into heavenly ones, in order to make sinners into saints; in order to raise us up from corruption into incorruption, from earth to heaven; from enslavement to sin and the devil — into the glorious freedom of children of God; from death — into immortality, in order to make us sons of God and to seat us together with him upon the throne as his royal children."

— *St. John of Kronstadt, Sermon on the Nativity of Christ*

Strength for Your Family

1. What is the underlying attitude of your family? How can it be further fostered or altered, depending on what it is?
2. In what is your family rooted?
3. Can you convince your children that they are "royal children of God"? How?

Strength for Your Soul

A Prayer to the Holy Spirit

Holy Spirit,
you are the soul of my soul.
I humbly adore you.
Enlighten me, strengthen me,
guide me, comfort me.
Reveal your wishes to me
as far as this is in accordance
with the will of the Eternal Father.
Show me what Eternal Love wants of me.
Show me what I should do.
Show me what I should suffer.
Show me what I should humbly and thoughtfully accept, bear, and endure.
Holy Spirit, show me your will
and the will of the Father,
for I want my whole life to be nothing else

than a continuous, an everlasting yes
to the wishes, to the will of God, the Eternal Father.
Amen.

*— Father Joseph Kentenich, Servant of God and founder of
the Schoenstatt Apostolic Movement,* Heavenwards,
American Edition, 1992 (used with permission)

Chapter Sixteen

BLUE BLOOD

*O*ur royalty shows in the way we attach ourselves to God, to our fellow men, and to creation; or how we detach ourselves from them. During the high Middle Ages, kingdoms and monarchies abounded. In a godly monarchy, the royal family was conscious of the fact that only God was above them. They understood that God is the supreme ruler and they were only his instruments. That's true for us, too. All that we have "under" us ultimately belongs to him, and so we try to govern ourselves and our families according to God's laws, discerning his will before we take any action of our own.

With that in mind, with whom did the royal family members attach themselves? Unless it's an act of charity, they likely would not have been hobnobbing with the lower classes. They kept themselves above the riffraff, in order to preserve their reputation and dignity. (Granted, some royalty has done this to excess and even cruelly in the past.) We, too, must rise above the riffraff in our lives — whether that's people, places, or things — that will drag us down into the scum of sin. Mark or I have often told our kids, "You are far too good for that!" We weren't suggesting that they're better than anybody else, or that they should turn their noses up at anyone who was less fortunate than themselves materially, intellectually, or spiritually. We were reminding them that they are cherished royal children of God and therefore should not lower themselves by associating with those who would attempt to mar their reputation and dignity with sinfulness.

We tried to convey to our children that our attitude toward sin has to be one of utter horror. Sin can't be something we just casually step around — it has to send us retching and reeling in the opposite direction. We have to see sin — even the smallest sin — as an obstacle to our relationship with God and a threat to our inheritance.

St. Maria Goretti exemplified this in the most beautiful way. When she was twelve years old, her eighteen-year-old neighbor attempted to rape her. He threatened to stab her with a knife if she did not submit. Her response was that she would rather die than offend God, and so he stabbed her, not once, but many times. She survived the attack, but not for long. While in the hospital, she forgave her attacker. Can we imagine forgiving someone who has brutally attacked us? Yet, this is what we're called to do as the King's royal children. Sin must repulse us, but at the same time forgiveness must motivate us.

Royal families on earth pass on their blue-blooded heritage to their children, including the lands, possessions, and privileges that come with it. We pass on our heritage to our children, too; a rich heritage that includes the privilege to call ourselves children of God and to share in his divine life. It's the heritage of our faith, given as a gift from God and passed on from generation to generation. It's the right to visit with the King in the throne room of our hearts, in our domestic church, and in the tabernacle that holds his real Presence. It's the heritage that allows us to walk with our heads held high in acknowledgment of our blessings.

Our greatest blessing is God's love for us, which is provident, compassionate, and heroic. It is provident in that he kindly and lovingly invites us to draw near to him. He tells us, "Come to me, all who labor and are heavy laden, and I will give you rest" (Mt 11:28). He is the Good Shepherd who will search to the ends of the earth for the lost lamb (see Lk 15:4). His love is compassionate in that he understands our needs and suffering completely. He heals us (Lk 6:6-10), casts out our demons (Mt 8:16), feeds us (Mt 15:36), and offers us forgiveness (Jn 8:7). His love is heroic in that he surrendered his honor, suffered unspeakable torment, and gave his life for us (Jn 15:13). He did all of this out of love for us.

The sacraments are part of the privilege of our royal heritage, and so we receive them as often as we can. Jesus stressed the importance of the sacraments when he said: "Abide in me and I in you. As the branch cannot bear fruit by itself, unless it abides in the vine, neither can you, unless you abide in me" (Jn 15:4).

Over the years, Mark and I have used the image of the domestic church to inspire our children, explaining to them that the Church — especially our little domestic church — has many different components, all essential to

ONE BODY IN ONE SPIRIT

"For just as the body is one and has many members, and all the members of the body, though many, are one, so it is with Christ. For by one Spirit we were all baptized into one body — Jews or Greeks, slaves or free — and all were made to drink of one Spirit. For the body does not consist of one member but of many."

— 1 Corinthians 12:12-14

make it a church. What do we find in a physical church? We find an altar, a tabernacle, crucifix, sanctuary lamp, candles, statues, pews, windows, doors, and so on. Without all of those things, the church would not be a church. We use these images to drive home the reality that the church needs each one of us, all of us, to be a church. So, too, Fenelon Clan needs each one of us, all of us to be Fenelon Clan. When the children reached a certain level of comprehension — anywhere from four to seven years old — we encouraged them to choose a symbol from the Church to "become." We would take them to our home shrine, let them look at the various items, and begin a dialogue with them about which symbol or symbols most attracted them. We encouraged each child to consider his or her symbol, thinking about what it represented in the larger church, what it represented in our little domestic church, and what it meant to them personally. What happened after that was fascinating and became like the question of which came first, the chicken or the egg. In each of our children, we observed that as they grew and developed, they internalized their symbol and became more and more like it.

For example, Luke chose to be the picture of the Blessed Virgin Mary we have in our domestic church. He's never been afraid of new situations or of letting people know what he thinks, and he's been called on in many situations to represent the Blessed Mother through his beliefs. When he enrolled in a sociology course at the local technical college, his "picture" really came to life. His instructor stood blatantly against everything we as Catholics stand for, not only in her own private belief system, but also and most especially in the ideologies that she forced upon her students. Even worse, if her students (namely Luke) turned in assignments that were contrary to her ideologies, they were given a poor grade even if it was quality work. As could be imagined, this led to some pretty fiery class discussions, including open ridicule of Luke for his belief system. The more the instructor tried to sway Luke from his thinking, the more firmly he stood ground! Did Luke choose the picture of the Blessed Virgin because he already had it in him, or did striving toward "becoming" the picture give him the gumption he needed for the future? We'll never know, but we're certainly glad for his choice, and so is he.

Strength for Your Spirit

"The Second Vatican Council describes the content of Christian education as follows: 'Such an education does not merely strive to foster maturity … in the human person. Rather, its principal aims are these: that as baptized persons are gradually introduced into a knowledge of the mystery of salvation, they may daily grow more conscious of the gift of faith which they have received; that they may learn to adore God the Father in spirit and in truth (cf. Jn 4:23), especially through liturgical worship; that they may be trained to conduct their personal life in true righteousness and holiness, according to their new nature (Eph 4:22-24), and thus grow to maturity, to the stature of the fullness of Christ (cf. Eph 4:13), and devote themselves to the upbuilding of the Mystical Body. Moreover, aware of their calling, they should grow accustomed to giving witness to the hope that is in them (cf. 1 Pt 3:15), and to promoting the Christian transformation of the world.'"

— *Blessed John Paul II,* Familiaris Consortio,
*"On the Role of the Christian Family
in the Modern World," 1981*

Strength for Your Family

1. To what or whom does your family attach itself?
2. What is your heritage? As a family? As Catholics?
3. How has God's providence led your family through the years? What are the outstanding moments in which you experienced his special care for you?
4. How, specifically, can your domestic church symbolize the universal Church?

Strength for Your Soul

Prayer for Guidance

O creator past all telling, you have appointed from the treasures

of your wisdom the hierarchies of angels,

disposing them in wondrous order above the bright heavens,

and have so beautifully set out all parts of the universe.

You we call the true fount of wisdom and the noble origin of all things.

Be pleased to shed on the darkness of mind in which I was born,

the twofold beam of your light and warmth to dispel my ignorance and sin.

You make eloquent the tongues of children.

Then instruct my speech and touch my lips with gra-
ciousness.

Make me keen to understand, quick to learn, able to
remember;

make me delicate to interpret and ready to speak.

Guide my going in and going forward, lead home
my going forth.

You are true God and true man, and live for ever and
ever.

Amen

Chapter Seventeen

DETACHED ATTACHMENTS

Working with symbols, especially when the children are young, is essential in helping them understand the doctrines and practices of our faith and in fostering the attachments necessary to become healthy, vibrant Catholic adults. This includes our attachment to God, but also our attachment to our fellow men and creation. True holiness involves not only the way we relate to God, but also the way we relate to people and things. We do this by forming attachments that are priestly, prophetic, and heroic, and following with what the Catechism teaches us about being a priestly, prophetic people. Then the people, events, and things around us become symbols to us of God's boundless love and tender care.

One of the most obvious ways we encounter God's love and care is through the people in our lives. St. Francis de Sales told those under his spiritual guidance that "we cannot always offer God great things, but at each instant we can offer him little things with great love." His spiritual advice included the practicing of "little virtues," those things whose practical application can form a pattern of holiness in us and in our children. These are the virtues of humility, patience, charity, kindness, forbearance, weakness, willingness, warmness and gentleness of heart, sympathy, forgiveness, simplicity, and sincerity.

Of these virtues St. Francis de Sales said:

"Everyone is eager to possess those brilliant, almost dazzling virtues which cluster round the summit of the Cross, so that they can be seen from afar and admired, but very few are anxious to gather those which, like wild thyme, grow at the foot of that Tree of Life and under its shade. Yet these are often the most hardy, and give out the sweetest perfume, being watered with the precious Blood of the Savior, whose first lesson to his disciples was: Learn of me because I am meek and humble of heart.

"It does not belong to everyone to practice the sublime virtues of fortitude, magnanimity, endurance unto death, patience, constancy, and courage. The occasions of exercising these are rare, yet all aspire to them because they are brilliant and their names high sounding. Very often, too, people fancy that they are able, even now, to practice them. They inflate their courage with the vain opinion they have of themselves, but when put to the trial fail pitiably. They are like those children of Ephrem, who distinguished themselves wonderfully by, in the time of peace, hitting the target with every arrow, but in the battle were the first to fly before the enemy. Better had their skill been less and their courage greater."

Unlimited opportunities to practice the little virtues arise in daily life, especially in our domestic church. While they're considered the smallest of virtues, they're certainly not the easiest.

Once, when I was sitting along the sideline of a gym class for our homeschool support group, two brothers got into a brawl over a football play. In their eagerness, they had collided and caused a fumble. Not surprisingly, each blamed the other for their error. They were shouting, and then pushing and shoving started. Their mom, also along the sideline, stepped in and broke up the fight.

"You two stop right now," she said sternly to the red-faced boys who stood there facing each other with their mother's hands firmly gripping their collars.

"Apologize to your brother," she insisted. The boys remained silent, huffing and puffing and glaring at each other. "Apologize!" she insisted again. This time she gave those collars a little twist.

"I'm sorry!" each shouted at the other. This was not quite the apologetic attitude their mother was looking for, and so she "suggested" that they come and sit with her for a few minutes while the rest of the young people continued the game.

My heart went out to this mom. It was a tough situation made even tougher by being in a public place. How many times have we faced similar situations with our own children? Those little virtues can require a big amount of effort.

Our Lord takes this a step further. "You have heard that it was said, 'An eye for an eye and a tooth for a tooth.' But I say to you, Do not resist one who is evil. But if any one strikes you on the right cheek, turn to him the other also; and if any one would sue you and take your coat, let him have cloak as well; and if any one forces you to go one mile, go with him two miles. Give to him who begs from you, and do not refuse him who would borrow from you" (Mt 5:38-42).

By serving our fellow man, we serve God, but we also can serve God through created things. As royal, priestly, prophetic people, we should look at the world differently.

GOD IN ALL

"A man cannot really be religious one hour, and not religious the next. We might as well say he could be in a state of good health one hour, and in bad health the next. A man who is religious, is religious morning, noon, and night; his religion is a certain character, a mold in which his thoughts, words, and actions are cast, all forming parts of one and the same whole. He sees God in all things; every course of action he directs towards those spiritual objects which God has revealed to him; every occurrence of the day, every event, every person met with, all news which he hears, he measures by the standard of God's will. And a person who does this may be said almost literally to pray without ceasing; for, knowing himself to be in God's presence, he is continually led to address him reverently, whom he sets always before him, in the inward language of prayer and praise, of humble confession and joyful trust."

— *Cardinal John Henry Newman,* Mental Prayers

In this light, we look at people and things prophetically, seeing them for their symbolic as well as practical value. St. Augustine called this *Nutus Dei,* or "hints from God." St. Bonaventure spoke of it as *manutergium Dei,* or the way we see God's footprints in daily life, leading us to his fatherly heart.

There is a restaurant in our area that advertises service that's "so fast you'll freak." Our kids, especially our daughter, like to tease me about having "freaky fast faith," because it seems to them that when I pray, I get whatever I want the instant I want it, just like the fast-food customers. Actually, my faith isn't any quicker or more ardent than anyone else's. It's only that I take the time to point out to our children those little prophets of God in daily life that pop up here and there and herald God's love for us.

One late summer night last year, I took our energetic little dog on a walk along the lakeshore. A stroll like that gives me some peace and quiet and allows my heart and mind to unravel the knots that get caught inside of them. On this particular night, it was kind of chilly, and I was really knotted up from a very tough week. Additionally, I still had a lot to do, with a mess of papers spread all over my desk. It was late, but I decided to take the pooch for a stroll anyway. I took a different route that night, which was extra refreshing.

After weaving my way back and forth through the neighborhood, I headed toward the lakeshore. It's strange, but even though I'm terrified of large bodies of water, I'm strongly attracted to the stretch of Lake Michigan close to my home. I can never get enough of tromping up and down those weatherworn asphalt paths that are supposed to make you feel as though you're really out in the wilderness somewhere. As I plod along, I envision myself taking a power walk along some lake that's way out in the middle of nowhere. In my imagination, I take the Blessed Mother with me, using the time for prayer and contemplation. That night I couldn't keep my eyes off the horizon. The way the greenish-blue of the lake met the grayish-blue of the sky had a somewhat mystifying effect. When I looked with a critical eye, it formed a crisp, clear line. When I settled back and let my eyes rest on the horizon, it had a kind of muted, undefined effect.

I stood still for a moment, just letting my eyes do whatever they wanted to do. I went from critical looking to restful gazing and back and forth between the two. It was amazing how the horizon changed depending upon whether I was examining it critically or just kind of taking it all in.

Suddenly, I was reminded of something I'd heard in a spiritual-mentoring class. The instructor used the image of the horizon to explain the faith journey and subsequent transformation of human beings. She said it's like standing at the lakeshore and looking at the horizon. You can see only so far, but it seems like you're looking all the way to the end, yet you know that all kinds of stuff lies beyond it. Sometimes, as you're watching, a ship appears and you wonder, "Now, where did that come from?" Then it passes by and is gone. Then, after a while, another ship appears and you wonder, "Well, where did that one come from?" and so it goes.

That's how my life is, I thought. I keep looking at the horizon, wanting to see all the way to the other side, but I can't. If I look too critically, I divide the sky (the Divine) from the lake (the human). I can't see how the two work together, because I've mechanistically separated them. If I just kind of restfully gaze back and forth between the two, it has a muted effect through which the Divine and human blend together. Maybe a ship comes, and maybe it doesn't, but it's all part of the same cohesive picture.

That's how those little prophets of God work; they're everyday people, things, and happenings that testify to the power and wonders of God and how they are at work in our lives.

Strength for Your Spirit

"God can use a book, a lover, a sickness or anything to draw us to the Deity. The Spirit can reach into the joints, imaginations and hearts of each soul uniquely when it pleases God. Sometimes we seek God ardently, but often we lose our first fervor. However, God is always seeking to touch and move us and to be our Guide and instruct us according to holy providence. The more we earnestly beg and beseech God, the more God hears us and reveals the divine presence mysteriously and devotionally within our soul. The more we pray, the more the Spirit prays with us to cooperate with God's plan and purpose not only for ourselves but for others, too. Gifts are always for sharing with all creations and especially God's creatures. It does not take a Doctor of the Church to convert us. The Almighty can use the most insignificant, the most deplorable or the most blessed to achieve divine results."

— *Abbot Dom John Eudes*

Strength for Your Family

1. By what means can you help your family to practice the little virtues? Which one could you begin working on immediately?
2. What does it mean for you to be a royal, priestly, prophetic family? What does that look like in practical terms?
3. How can you allow your faith to permeate every aspect of life?

Strength for Your Soul

A Family Consecration

O God of goodness and mercy, to your fatherly guidance we commend our family, our household and all our belongings. We commit all to your love and keeping; fill this house with your blessings even as you filled the holy House of Nazareth with your presence.

Keep far from us, above all else, the blemish of sin, and reign in our midst by your law, by your most holy love and by the exercise of every Christian virtue. Let each one of us obey you, love you, and set himself to follow in his own life your example, that of Mary, your mother, and our most loving Mother, and that of your blameless guardian, Saint Joseph.

Protect us and our house from all evils and misfortunes, but grant that we may be always resigned to your divine will even in the sorrows which you send us. Finally give all of us the grace to live in perfect harmony and in the fullness of love toward our neighbor. Grant that every one of us may deserve by a holy life the comfort of your holy sacraments at the hour of death. O Jesus, bless us and protect us.

O Mary, Mother of grace and of mercy, defend us against the wicked spirit, reconcile us with your Son, commit us to his keeping, that so we may be made worthy of his promises.

Saint Joseph, foster-father of our Savior, guardian of his holy mother, head of the Holy Family, intercede for us, bless us and defend our home at all times.

Saint Michael, defend us against all the evil cunning of hell.

Saint Gabriel, make us to understand the holy will of God.

Saint Raphael, preserve us from all sickness and from every danger to our lives.

Our holy Guardian Angels, keep our feet safely on the path of salvation both day and night.

Our holy Patrons, pray for us before the throne of God.

Bless this house, O God the Father, who created us; O God the Son, who suffered for us on the holy Cross; and O Holy Spirit, who sanctified us in holy baptism. May the one God in three divine Persons preserve our bodies, purify our minds, direct our hearts, and bring us all to everlasting life.

Glory be to the Father, glory be to the Son, glory be to the Holy Spirit! Amen.

Chapter Eighteen

GOD'S AWESOME CREATION

As we grow in holiness, we learn not only to listen to the "little prophets" that come into our lives, but also we respond to them by turning to God and opening our minds and hearts to his will. Then, we can go a step further. We praise God through his creation just as the priest does at Mass. The priest takes the gifts in the name of the people and offers them to God, praising him for his glory and goodness. Creation, then, becomes the means by which we praise God.

Just before Matt was deployed the last time, Fenelon Clan traveled to El Paso, Texas, to spend a few last days with him before he shipped out. We had a great time seeing all the sights and exploring the landscape. El Paso is in a mountainous area; everywhere you look, you can see flat stretches of desert surrounded by mountain ranges. On one of our day trips, we stopped at a viewing area overlooking an expansive valley in between the mountains. At first, I was really intimidated by the height of the mountains and the depths of the valley, especially since there was nothing but a metal pole fence between me and the abyss. But the color was so beautiful I couldn't help but look. I was glad I did. As I stood there and realized that God in his greatness had created this amazing scene, I thanked him for his generosity. It dawned on me that only God in his mightiness would create something this awesome. Additionally, I realized that the same God who had the power to create these mountains and valleys had the power to protect the soldiers overseas and bring Matt home safely. When Matt did return safely almost a year later, I remembered the scenic view, and I praised God again.

We all have moments like that in our life in which we find ourselves in awe of God's creation. These are opportune times to share with our children, pointing out God's goodness and power and praising him together. It's more of a challenge on a daily basis, but we can do it.

Don't we often forget about all the little things for which we can offer praise during the day? Instead of cursing the heat, praise God for the way the sunlight reflects his tender care for growing things. Instead of listening to our children gripe about their homework, help them to offer praise to God for the opportunity to exercise the intellect he's graciously given them. Everything we touch, ev-

CREATION AS GIFT

"'And God saw everything he had made and behold it was very good' (Gn 1:31).

This ancient text, so simple and yet so profound, is a reminder to all of us today that the world we live in, this creation, is to be seen and embraced by all people in its totality as good: good because it is a gift from God: good because it is the environment in which all of us have been placed and in which we are called to live out our vocations in solidarity with one another."

— *Pope Paul VI, Worldwide Day of Environment, June 5, 1977*

erything we own, everything we use, everyone we know, and even our very selves should elicit in us a spontaneous song of praise. Then, we offer these things back to God — as the priest does during Mass — thereby making them a holy and pleasing sacrifice.

St. Francis of Assisi was an absolute master at this. In his famous "Canticle of the Sun," written in 1225, he offers God praise for all creation. Notice how he accepts the world around him as a gift from God and then in a priestly way offers them back to God:

> Most high, all powerful, all good Lord! All praise is yours, all glory, all honor, and all blessing. To you, alone, Most High, do they belong. No mortal lips are worthy to pronounce your name.

> Be praised, my Lord, through all your creatures, especially through my lord Brother Sun, who brings the day; and you give light through him. And he is beautiful and radiant in all his splendor! Of you, Most High, he bears the likeness.

> Be praised, my Lord, through Sister Moon and the stars; in the heavens you have made them, precious and beautiful.

> Be praised, my Lord, through Brothers Wind and Air, and clouds and storms, and all the weather, through which you give your creatures sustenance.

> Be praised, My Lord, through Sister Water; she is very useful, and humble, and precious, and pure.

> Be praised, my Lord, through Brother Fire, through whom you brighten the night. He is beautiful and cheerful, and powerful and strong.

Be praised, my Lord, through our sister Mother Earth, who feeds us and rules us, and produces various fruits with colored flowers and herbs.

Be praised, my Lord, through those who forgive for love of you; through those who endure sickness and trial. Happy those who endure in peace, for by you, Most High, they will be crowned.

Be praised, my Lord, through our Sister Bodily Death, from whose embrace no living person can escape. Woe to those who die in mortal sin! Happy those she finds doing your most holy will. The second death can do no harm to them.

Praise and bless my Lord, and give thanks, and serve him with great humility.

Strength for Your Spirit

"For there is no one so uncivilized, and of such uncultivated disposition, who, when he raises his eyes to heaven, although he knows not by the providence of what God all this visible universe is governed, does not understand from the very magnitude of the objects, from their motion, arrangement, constancy, usefulness, beauty, and temperament, that there is some Providence, and that that which exists with wonderful method must have been prepared by some greater intelligence."

— *Lacantius,* Divine Institutes

Strength for Your Family

1. Have you ever experienced a time when you were completely in awe of God's creation? What was that like?
2. How can you recapture that feeling and allow it to help you see the world around you in a new light?
3. What steps can you take to foster an overall attitude of gratefulness in your family?

Strength for Your Soul

Prayer of Gratitude

Thank you, Father, for having created us and given us to each other in the human family.

Thank you for being with us in all our joys and sorrows, for your comfort in our sadness, your companionship in our loneliness.

Thank you for yesterday, today, tomorrow and for the whole of our lives.

Thank you for friends, for health and for grace. May we live this and every day conscious of all that has been given to us.

— The Catholic Prayer Book,
compiled by Msgr. Michael Buckley

Chapter Nineteen

NECESSITIES OF LIFE

*O*ur holiness also depends on the way we use the things that God gives us. We want to employ them in a heroic way, with a divine indifference that creates a balance between attachment and detachment. This is a bit tricky because often we are exteriorly dependent on things out of necessity. We need a home for our family, and income by which we provide for our needs. In most cases, a car is necessary for transportation, books are necessary for education, and so on. We can't do without material things, but we can foster an attitude of independence from them. We can also foster an attitude of independence from physical comfort, honor, esteem, and pleasures of the senses.

Our Lord, of course, was the best example for us. He was poor, humble, and meek, and — in the end — lost all his honor and was crucified as a common criminal. As he told his disciples, "Foxes have holes, and birds of the air have nests; but the Son of man has nowhere to lay his head" (Lk 9:58). As the King of Kings, he could have had anything he wanted at the snap of a finger. Instead, he renounced all of it for our sakes, beginning from the first moment of his birth when he was laid in a manger's cold wood in a stable in Bethlehem. At the end of his life, he again was laid on cold wood: the cross of the Crucifixion. He sought nothing for himself but to follow the will of his heavenly Father. By his words and actions, the Savior is

NOT BUT GOD...

My God,
Not the intellect, but God;
Not the will, but God;
Not the soul, but God;
Not hearing, but God;
Not smell, but God;
Not taste and speech, but God;
Not breath, but God;
Not feeling, but God;
Not the heart, but God;
Not the body, but God;
Not the air, but God;
Not food and drink, but God;
Not clothing, but God;
Not repose, but God;
Not earthly goods, but God;
Not riches, but God;
Not honors, but God;
Not distinctions, but God;
Not dignities, but God;
Not promotions, but God;
God in all and always.

— *St. Vincent Palloti*

telling us that nothing is more important than God and no person or thing should ever come between our heavenly Father and us.

Again, the beatitudes become the framework of our lives. The humility, self-denial, and love they profess become the foundation for our heroic attachment to the people, happenings, places, and things around us. The only things we should actually "crave" are holiness, purity of heart, mercy, peace, and joy. For us, only God should matter.

If we would live St. Vincent Pallotti's prayer, we would become perfectly detached from the world and perfectly attached to God! This is the attitude for which all Christians strive, and for which we strive in our domestic church.

A friend of ours has been an exceptional example for us of heroic attachment and detachment. He owned his own transport business, having built it from the ground up. The company grew, and so did the responsibilities and subsequently the hours he needed to put in to make it run. This put stress on his family, because of the long hours of his absence and because he was always stressed out himself. Finally, enough was enough; he made the decision to close down the business. (Trying to sell it would have taken even more time and energy away from his family.) At that point, he didn't even have any solid job prospects, but he knew that facing temporary unemployment was a lot better than the burden his business was placing on his family. He closed the business, and started fresh — all for the sake of his family and in keeping with what he discerned to be God's will. Not long after, he found a job, and now his family is much better off than they were when he owned his own business.

We shouldn't throw caution to the wind and give up essentials or put our families in danger just because things start to get tough. We must do what is necessary for the health and safety of our family, but we must be willing to let the rest pass away should God require it. He will only require that which is good for us. Therefore, we take reasonable care of our temporal needs, with confidence in God's fatherly goodness.

We can show our children how to do this in the little things around the house. For example, do we absolutely have to have it toasty warm in the house in winter? Could we turn the thermostat down just a bit and sacrifice our comfort for the love of God? In summer, could we turn the air conditioner down a few degrees and dare to sweat a bit? It's more difficult to detach ourselves from things we particularly love. When a child's favorite toy breaks, it's not going to work to just tell him he should heroically detach himself and let it go. But, for example, if we set an example ourselves of not getting bent out of shape when the Internet is down, our children will gradually learn how to conquer their own frustrations and become detached from the world in order to attach themselves to God.

Strength for Your Spirit

"If God sends you adversity, accept it with patience and give thanks for it to Our Lord, realizing that you have deserved it and that it will be for your own good. If he gives you prosperity, thank him humbly for it, so that the gift which should improve you may not, through pride or in any other way, make you worse; or, one should not use God's gifts to war against him."

— *St. Louis IX of France*

Strength for Your Family

1. What is "divine indifference"? How can you begin to live that in daily life?

2. What are your real necessities? In what ways could you simplify your lifestyle?
3. It isn't easy to completely trust God for our temporal needs. How can you spiritually prepare yourselves to undertake that kind of trust?

Strength for Your Soul

Act of Abandonment
Father,
I abandon myself into your hands;
do with me whatever you will.
Whatever you may do, I thank you;
I am ready for all, I accept all.
Let only your will be done in me,
and in all your creatures.
I wish no more than this, O Lord.
Into your hands I commend my spirit;
I offer it to you with all the love of my heart,
for I do love you, Lord, and so need to give myself,
to surrender myself into your hands,
without reserve, and with boundless confidence,
for you are my Father.

— *Charles de Foucald*

Chapter Twenty

STEWARDSHIP

When we look at the things around us in a priestly, prophetic, and heroic way and help our children to do the same, we enable and ennoble them to become truly holy Christian people — a royal people. This is what the Church refers to as stewardship.

More and more as a culture we view work as a means to our own selfish aims instead of a means to praise and glorify God. As the United States Conference of Catholic Bishops said in its "Stewardship: A Disciple's Response":

> "This human activity of cultivating and caring has a generic name: work. It is not a punishment for or a consequence of sin. True, sin does painfully skew the experience of work: 'By the sweat of your face shall you get bread to eat' (Gn 3:19). But, even so, God's mandate to humankind to collaborate with him in the task of creating — the command to work — comes before the Fall. Work is a fundamental aspect of the human vocation. It is necessary for human happiness and fulfillment. It is intrinsic to responsible stewardship of the world."

Children, of course, don't necessarily see it that way, and that's why I blew a gasket during chore time one day when the kids were younger. I had had enough of their complaining and foot-dragging and just wanted to get the work done so we could move on with our day. So I left them to themselves and disappeared into the home office

STEWARDSHIP AND FAITH

"Man was created in God's image and was commanded to conquer the earth and to rule the world in justice and holiness: he was to acknowledge God as maker of all things and relate himself and the totality of creation to him, so that through the dominion of all things by man the name of God would be majestic in all the earth.

"Christian theology uses both domestic and royal imagery to describe this special role. Employing royal imagery, it is said that human beings are called to rule in the sense of holding an ascendancy over the whole of visible creation, in the manner of a king. But the inner meaning of this kingship is, as Jesus reminds his disciples, one of service: only by willingly suffering as a sacrificial victim does Christ become the king of the universe, with the Cross as his throne. Employing domestic imagery, Christian theology speaks of man as the master of a household to whom God has confided care of all his goods (cf. Mt 24:45)."

— Communion and Worship:
Human Persons Created in the Image of God,
International Theological Commission

with my Bible. After a few minutes of flipping through St. Paul's letters, I found the passage for which I was looking:

"For even when we were with you, we gave you this command: If any one will not work, let him not eat" (2 Thes 3:10). I got out my nice, fat, black marker and scrawled the words on the biggest piece of paper we had in the house. Then, I hung it on the wall just outside the bathroom door. Since they all strongly disliked cleaning the bathroom, I figured that was the perfect place for the sign.

Matt, then a preteen, was the first to see it. "Oh, gimme a break," he said sarcastically.

"You can't do that!" Monica said, and stomped her foot.

Luke's eyes were wide in fearful anticipation.

"You think I'm kidding?" I countered. "Try me."

Lunchtime came and went with the chores still not being completely done. As suppertime approached and the children's stomachs started to growl more loudly, they began to consider the possibility that I really did mean what St. Paul said. They finally finished the chores, and we sat down to supper. I was truly grateful because I had no idea what I would do if they had continued the strike.

This might seem to be an extreme tactic, but Mark and I highly value work, and we want our children to highly value it also, for the good of the household, but even more so for their own good and the glory of God. We show our love for God and our fellow man through the work that we do. Any work that draws us closer to God and fellow man is "good" work; any work that draws us away from God and fellow man (especially our families) is "bad" work.

Therefore, work is not only a physical activity; it's a spiritual one as well. When we put our hands to the plow, so to speak, in the spirit of self-sacrifice, we work both with and for God. This is true not only of manual labor, such as household chores, but also the work that we do profession-ally and apostolically. Libraries throughout the country have shelves filled with books addressing the extent and severity of "workaholism." Why? It's because our attitude toward work has been twisted by ungodly influences.

For several years, our kids have shoveled snow for an elderly neighbor. As the older child moved on to other things, the next one in line took his or her place. The kids have always looked forward to the extra cash, and I've looked forward to getting them outside for some exercise in the cold winter months. As they each took their turns, I've "strongly encouraged" them to give our neighbor at least one freebie service. The initial reaction was always a raised eyebrow; after they thought about it, they realized it was a good idea and gladly did it out of service for God and neighbor. Work is good for the heart as well as the pocketbook!

The Rule of St. Benedict includes the encouragement *ora et labora* (pray and work). There is more to this often-quoted adage than meets the eye. Obviously, prayer and work are beneficial, especially when both are lifted up to God with a sincere heart. But St. Benedict had something else in mind when he told his monks to work and pray: their mental and emotional well-being. St. Benedict knew that the austere monastery life in which they lived could easily lead his brothers to depression and even despair if they did not keep their hands busy and their minds and hearts focused on God.

Strength for Your Spirit

"To be active in works and unfaithful in heart is like raising a beautiful and lofty building on an unsound foundation. The higher the building, the greater the fall. Without the support of faith, good works cannot stand."

— *St. Ambrose*

Strength for Your Family

1. What kind of stewards are you? Of your possessions? Your time? Your resources?
2. How can you become examples of holy stewardship for your children?
3. What is your attitude toward work? Does it need an adjustment? How?
4. What can you do to show your children the godly value of work?

Strength for Your Soul

Prayer of St. Benedict

Gracious and Holy Father,
Grant us the intellect to understand you,
reason to discern you,
diligence to seek you,
wisdom to find you,
a spirit to know you,
a heart to meditate upon you.
May our ears hear you,
may our eyes behold you
and may our tongues praise you.
Give us grace that our way of life may be pleasing to you,
that we may have the patience to wait for you,
and the perseverance to look for you.
Grant us a perfect end:
your Holy Presence,
a blessed resurrection and life everlasting.
We ask this through Jesus Christ our Lord. Amen.

Chapter Twenty-One

JOY IN SUFFERING

W e're called to imitate Christ in every aspect, and that includes in his suffering. Suffering is part of the human condition and an essential part of our Christian life. St. Paul said, "Now I rejoice in my suffering for your sake, and in my flesh I complete what is lacking in Christ's afflictions for the sake of his body, that is, the church " (Col 1:24). He isn't suggesting that Christ's suffering is remiss; he's pointing out that God seeks our willing participation as members of the Mystical Body.

The fact is that we will always have some kind of suffering, and there's nothing we can do to change that. We can, however, change our attitude toward suffering.

When my sister-in-law was pregnant with her daughter, prenatal testing showed that the baby likely would be born with serious anomalies if the baby even survived the pregnancy and birth. Needless to say, this was quite a blow for the parents, but also for the entire extended family. During a pause in a conversation with my sister-in-law, I, half-thinking, uttered a rhetorical question, "Don't you just wonder why?"

"No, Margaret," she said to me. "I don't see it that way at all. I don't ask, why me. I ask, why *not* me? If God wants this suffering of me then I will gladly give it to him."

My sister-in-law's response still rests in my heart and is a tremendous source of inspiration for me. My niece was indeed born with many, many difficulties and has endured a number of painful surgeries already in her young life; there will be more ahead for her. But she has spunk, spirit, and a zest for life that most of us without any difficulties at all could hardly hope to obtain. And her parents have walked the path — joyfully — right along with her. This is the lesson that we must teach our children: to ask why *not* me in regard to suffering.

The case of my niece is obviously an exceptional one, but we can teach our children to accept suffering by beginning with the little things in life. Could we wait a little longer before reaching for the aspirin bottle when we have a headache? A scraped knee can be put togreat use when it's offered for the souls in purgatory. Job loss, family strife, insults, misunderstandings, any kind of hardship can be seen as little prophets of God calling us to greater imitation of Christ, deeper spiritual growth, and opportunities to offer priestly, royal sacrifice to God. Our lives could be made so much richer if we could learn to accept suffering in humility, bear it in patience, and offer it in joy.

This was the great charism of the Holy Family. They lived an attitude of joyful surrender to the heavenly Father at all times, in all things, including suffering. By joy, we don't mean the giddy kind of happiness that we experience when we open a birthday present. Rather we mean that kind of deep, inner peace and delight that comes from resting in the possession of a good. It's the difference between pulling through the drive-in on a hot summer day and ordering an ice-cold beverage and spending a back-breaking day painting the family room. The drink is satisfying, delightful, and makes you happy. The painting takes sacrifice but gives you satisfaction in a job well done

THE NEW LAW OF THE SPIRIT

"Thus, the Christian family is inspired and guided by the new law of the Spirit and, in intimate communion with the Church, the kingly people, it is called to exercise its 'service' of love towards God and towards its fellow human beings. Just as Christ exercises His royal power by serving us, so also the Christian finds the authentic meaning of his participation in the kingship of his Lord in sharing his spirit and practice of service to man. 'Christ has communicated this power to his disciples that they might be established in royal freedom and that by self-denial and a holy life they might conquer the reign of sin in themselves' (cf. Rom 6:12). Further, he has shared this power so that by serving him in their fellow human beings they might through humility and patience lead their brothers and sisters to that King whom to serve is to reign. For the Lord wishes to spread his kingdom by means of the laity also, a kingdom of truth and life, a kingdom of holiness and grace, a kingdom of justice, love and peace. In this kingdom, creation itself will be delivered out of its slavery to corruption and into the freedom of the glory of the children of God (cf. Rom 8:21)."

— *Blessed John Paul II*, Familiaris Consortio,
"On the Role of the Christian Family
in the Modern World," 1981

and joy in serving your family and, through your family, God. That's how the Holy Family lived — ever joyful because they possessed the life of God. The source of their joy was seeing and serving God in the world around them.

That's our calling, too.

Strength for Your Spirit

"We all suffer for each other, and gain by each other's sufferings; for man never stands alone here, although he will stand by himself one day hereafter; but here he is a social being, and goes forward to his long home as one of a large company."

— Cardinal John Newman,
An Essay in Aid of a Grammar of Assent

Strength for Your Family

1. What are some moments of suffering in your history as a couple? as a family?
2. How did those times help you to grow? What good resulted from them?
3. How can you cultivate a spirit of joyful suffering in your family?
4. What does it mean to participate in the kingship of Our Lord? What does that look like on a practical level, in your daily lives?

Strength for Your Soul

With Heartfelt Love
With heartfelt love, I thank you, Mother dear,
with you to guide me, I need have no fear.
When all around seemed dark and drear and gray,
you stood as beacon for a brighter day.
Your smile illumined every wakeful hour,
You did uphold me with your gentle power.

Thanks, a thousand thanks to you, to God shall be now and for all eternity. Amen.

— Father Joseph Kentenich, Servant of God
and founder of the Schoenstatt Apostolic Movement,
used with permission,
Heavenwards, *American Edition, 1992*

Chapter Twenty-Two

ON WHOSE AUTHORITY?

*O*ur son Luke had landed a job with an internationally known security firm. It was his first "serious" job — one with benefits and real potential for advancement. He was very excited about it, and we were very excited for him. With this job, however, he was contracted to work at various sites and for various events.

Unfortunately, Planned Parenthood is one of this security firm's clients, and they asked Luke to assist in security outside of one of the clinics and at one of the events. When he mentioned this, I was aghast at the very thought of him having anything to do with the organization or any of its employees. I also was concerned about the image it would present and the message it would give to others who might see him at one of the sites or events. I gave him the rundown of Planned Parenthood's agenda and the moral dangers of being drawn into it. This wasn't anything new to Luke, he'd heard it all before from both Mark and me.

What was new for Luke was the moral dilemma I proposed to him: by protecting their sites and programs, he was assisting in their mission.

Luke, on the other hand, saw it in a completely different light. First of all, his concern was that in a time of economic crisis and exceptionally tight job market, he didn't have much choice. If he turned down assignments, he would likely find himself back on the job hunt. Even more, he thought of this as an opportunity to touch the hearts of those involved. "Think of it this way, Mom," he said. "Who would you rather have standing there on guard? Someone who supports what these people are doing, or someone like me who can look them in the eye and let them know that what they are doing is wrong? Not only that, but then I can be right there praying for each of the people as they come and go."

I understood where he was coming from, but I still had misgivings. On the other hand, he's an adult and capable of making his own decisions. "Okay, I disagree with this, but you're going to have to make up your own mind about it," I said.

He did. A few days later, he told me he had spoken with his supervisor, explaining to her the moral dilemma for him in guarding the Planned Parenthood sites because of his Catholic faith. She seemed somewhat surprised and then confided that she, too, was Catholic and understood Luke's position. She promised that she would discontinue the Planned Parenthood assignments as soon as she could find a substitute. Before long, Luke was transitioned into new sites, and the dilemma was solved.

Mark and I have found that couples tend to do one of two things when their children are faced with moral choices and are tempted to make decisions with which they don't agree: either they jump on the kid and try to force him into their way of thinking, or they simply look the other way. Neither is truly effective. Force only sends them running in the opposite direction, and avoidance sends the false message that what they're doing is permissible. Both choices are an abdication of our responsibility as parents; our job is to raise our children to have full and well-formed Christian consciences. That takes time, patience, diligence, encouragement, and, frequently, some serious nail-biting.

Consciences are developed, not dictated, and formed by authority. Authentic, godly authority is far different from the bosslike authority with which most of us are familiar. When we refer to authority within the domestic church, we're actually referring to leadership. As parents, we lead the way through our own example and guidance, always looking to God as the primary authority in our lives. If our children see us accepting God's authority in love and humility, they'll be able to accept our authority in like fashion. If they see us making informed and moral decisions based on sound Christian conscience, they will learn to do the same.

The Church uses the term "awaken" in the perfect sense. We want to awaken in our children prudence and

THE ROLE OF PARENTS IN FORMING CONSCIENCE

"The education of the conscience is a lifelong task. From the earliest years, it awakens the child to the knowledge and practice of the interior law recognized by conscience. Prudent education teaches virtue; it prevents or cures fear, selfishness and pride, resentment arising from guilt, and feelings of complacency, born of human weakness and faults. The education of the conscience guarantees freedom and engenders peace of heart."

— *Catechism of the Catholic Church (1784)*

right judgment so that they make purposeful choices rather than follow along blindly or out of fear.

I will never forget the scene I witnessed in a grocery store some years ago. John was just a baby, and Luke was preschool age. The store was crowded, and it was getting towards lunchtime. The woman behind me was obviously exasperated with the situation and with her children. Apparently, her toddler had wet his pants, and she was unhappy with him. I tried to ignore the motion behind me but could no longer resist when I heard her yelling at the child and referencing my Luke in her scolding. "Look at that, you blankety-blank!" She ridiculed. "You're a mess!" The little boy was crying pathetically and obviously scared. Pointing to Luke, she said, "I'll bet that little boy there never pees his pants!"

I drew Luke closer to me, and whispered in his ear: "It's okay, don't worry. She won't hurt you. She's just really mad right now. When we get in the car, we'll say a prayer for that family."

The checker finished our order, and we packed up and headed for the door. All the while, I could hear the mother berating her little boy, and my heart absolutely broke for him. With tears in my eyes, I loaded my kids and groceries in the car. On the way home, we said three Hail Mary's for this family, and I begged our Blessed Mother to somehow change the heart of that mother.

This is an extreme case, but it shows us how devastating force and ridicule can be for our children. That's not authority; it's bullying. While all of us lose our temper from time to time and say or do things more forcefully than we would like, we continue to strive for a stable, holy authority according to our God-given responsibility as parents. Ultimately, what we want is to be a reflection of

God's authority so that after our children become adults it will feel natural for them to follow him.

Our Lord has given us an excellent example of rightful authority: let the greatest among you become as the youngest, and the leader as one who serves. "For which is the greater, one who sits at table, or one who serves? Is it not the one who sits at table? But I am among you as one who serves" (Lk 22:27).

Let's look at motherliness and fatherliness again, this time in respect to the exercise of authority.

The father is the primary authority in the family. He provides security and community because he is the central figure of the family. As priest of the family, he preaches the Word of God by his life and example and helps his children to understand the world and the teaching of God. Like the priest, he remains open for his children, humble to admit that he too can fail, ready to serve, ready to forgive, and ready to look after his flock as a good shepherd. As priest, the father is anchored in the spiritual world and is not influenced by public opinion.

The father's role as priest also gives him the privilege and duty to bless his children. Blessing our children with holy water each day shows them that we take holiness seriously, protects them from the Evil One, and demonstrates our love and concern for both their bodies and their souls. It's best to get into this habit when the kids are young, but it's never too late!

An exemplary father also is an exemplary child. No one can be a true father who is not at the same time a true child of the heavenly Father. This isn't the same as child-*ish*ness, which is the result of immaturity. This is child-*like*ness, which is the result of religious roots and trust in God the Father. Look at Our Lord; he was a man of strong character, and yet he turned to the heavenly Father in all circumstances of his life. In a very manly way, he acknowledged the position and power of the Father. Just as Our Lord, the father of the family does nothing on his own authority, but rather by the authority God has given him. "I can do nothing on my own authority; as I hear, I judge; and my judgment is just, because I seek not my own will but the will of him who sent me. If I bear witness to myself, my testimony is not true; there is another who bears witness to me, and I know that the testimony which he bears to me is true" (Jn 5:30-32).

Finally, the father is the mirror of God the Father for his family. Without this dimension, the child will have a much more difficult time forming a relationship with the heavenly Father. Anyone who hasn't experienced fatherly love on a natural level can have a much harder time experiencing it on a supernatural level. So, fathers must work hard to reflect the heavenly Father as Jesus did. "Jesus said to him, 'Have I been with you so long, and yet you do not know me, Philip? He who has seen me has seen the Father; how can you say, "Show us the Father"? Do you not believe that I am in the Father and the Father in me? The words that I say to you I do not speak on my own authority; but the Father who dwells in me does his works'" (Jn 14:9-10).

Motherly authority is as critical as fatherly authority, but in a different way. Motherly authority must be careful not to overshadow fatherly authority. With more working and single mothers, this can easily happen. Add to that the push for fatherless children with the advent of *in vitro* fertilization, single motherhood, lesbian adoption, and surrogate motherhood, and we've got the makings of a real identity crisis for fathers.

The Blessed Mother shows mothers the way with her own being and actions. She shows her complete trust in the heavenly Father even when nothing makes sense, humanly speaking. The angel Gabriel told her that she is "full of grace," meaning that she is completely free of original sin and rests in God's favor. Then he told her that she'll become pregnant without having had relations with a man. What does she respond? "And Mary said, 'Behold, I am the handmaid of the Lord; let it be to me according to your word.' And the angel departed from her" (Lk 1:38).

Those words should resound constantly in the heart of every mother. Her motherly authority is a gift from God and a witness to his mercy and goodness. Mary exemplified this when she stood at the foot of the cross and accepted her spiritual motherhood. From then on, she would be mother, not just of Jesus, but of every human being for time eternal.

A mother's authority is based on her maternal qualities. That includes not only motherliness, but also the art of mediation. The mother mediates between father and child, between God and family. On a natural level, the mother introduces the child to the father. She's carried the child in her womb for nine months and upon birth, she presents him to the father. From then on she bears the responsibility of helping the relationship to deepen and grow. Because she has more contact with the child, the mother knows the child better and therefore can help the father to know the child better, too. The same takes place on the supernatural level.

Like Mary, mothers also mediate through their suffering. Men can endure great pain and difficulty, but women have a greater aptitude for long-suffering. The mother freely surrenders her own comfort — whether physical or emotional — for the sake of the family. We know that Mary did this under the cross and continues to do it today, as has been proven by the various apparitions, especially at Fátima.

Through our baptism, we're called to be royal, priestly parents to our children, exercising our God-given authority with kindness and benevolence. When we truly understand the essence of our authority, we can be leaders and nurturers of our children and help them to become the nurturers and leaders of the future.

Strength for Your Spirit

"Educate youth to obedience and respect for authority. This is simple when man is submissive to God and recognizes that absolute value of his commandments. For the unbeliever and the man who denies God, there cannot be any true, just and ordered authority because there exists no authority except from God. Man can neither rule nor be ruled by fear and force."

— Pope Pius XII, Address to the Women
of Italian Catholic Action, July 24, 1949

Strength for Your Family

1. What is your idea of rightful authority?
2. How can you demonstrate rightful authority for your children?
3. What practical means can you use to lead your children toward a well-formed conscience?
4. What practical means can you use to awaken in your children prudence and right judgment?

5. How can your family help Dad to more closely mirror the heavenly Father and Mom mirror the Blessed Mother? What are some basic steps you can take toward those goals?

Strength for Your Soul

Prayer in Trust of God's Will

O God,
early in the morning I cry to you. Help me to pray and to concentrate my thoughts on you: I cannot do this alone. In me there is darkness, but with you there is light. I am lonely, but you do not leave me. I am feeble in heart, but with you there is help. I am restless, but with you there is peace. In me there is bitterness, but with you there is patience. I do not understand your ways, but you know the way for me.... Restore me to liberty, and enable me so to live now that I may answer before you and before me. Lord, whatever this day may bring, your name be praised.

Amen.

— Dietrich Bonhoeffer (composed in a Nazi prison while awaiting his execution)

Chapter Twenty-Three

BORN FREE

While working out at the YMCA the other day, I caught a show on the history channel about the "radical '60s." The program spoke of the rebelliousness of the time, the drive for freedom, and the proliferation of communes, especially on the West Coast. The communes seemed to offer young people everything they would ever want: free food, lodging, sex, and drugs; and freedom from laws, politics, religion, and anything else that would place constraints on their will.

I found the segment on Timothy Leary to be especially intriguing and alarming all at once. Leary was a noted psychologist and researcher at Harvard University who studied the effects of the hallucinogenic drug LSD (lysergic acid diethylamide) on more than three hundred fellow professors, graduate students, writers, philosophers, and clergymen. The formal goal of the 1961 study was to scientifically prove that psychedelic drugs could alter human behavior for the better. Leary's personal goal for the study was to "discover and make love with God, self, and woman."

Leary described the effects of LSD as the "greatest ecstasy that man has known; the ecstasy of revelation." At that time, LSD was legal, and he was so enamored by it that he began using it himself and opened a commune in a Millbrook, New York, estate where sex and drugs flowed freely. This lifestyle caught on rapidly and soon became a subculture — the "Psychedelic Movement" — of sex;

drugs; music ("acid rock" gained its title from LSD use by both performers and audience members); and drug-induced, pseudo-religious experiences. Leary referred to himself under the influence of LSD as "God intoxicated," and since he frequently used the drug, he was frequently "intoxicated."

Watching the video clips of the commune rituals and drug parties made me very sad for those young people. They threw off everything — the "establishment," social mores, the Church, their parents, their morals, and even their clothes. They were desperately searching for happiness and wanted to be free, but the freedom to which they were flocking would serve only to further enslave them and make them even more unhappy. Their hearts were yearning for love and fulfillment; little did they realize that those things can be found only in God. They were caught in a web of deception.

Kids today are still caught in that web, only now it's taken on a slightly different form through gangs, sex, and porn addiction, and the mesmerizing lure of technology, especially digital communication and social networking that separate them from God and man rather than drawing them into the community of believers. Only the love and grace of God can fill their souls, only his sacraments can feed them. There can be no freedom without God.

Our kids sometimes want to throw off everything and be free. The problem is, they have no idea what real freedom is unless we show it to them. We know that the ultimate source of freedom is God, but how does that look on a practical level? In its wonderful "Instruction on Christian Freedom and Liberation," the Congregation for the Doctrine of the Faith says this:

Far from being achieved in total self-sufficiency and an absence of relationships, freedom only truly exists where reciprocal bonds, governed by truth and justice, link people to one another. But for such

A FREE PERSONALITY

"God did not create man as a 'solitary being' but wished him to be a 'social being.' Social life therefore is not exterior to man: he can only grow and realize his vocation in relation with others. Man belongs to different communities: the family and professional and political communities, and it is inside these communities that he must exercise his responsible freedom. A just social order offers man irreplaceable assistance in realizing his free personality. On the other hand, an unjust social order is a threat and an obstacle which can compromise his destiny. In the social sphere, freedom is expressed and realized in actions, structures and institutions, thanks to which people communicate with one another and organize their common life. The blossoming of a free personality, which for every individual is a duty and a right, must be helped and not hindered by society. Here we have an exigency of a moral nature which has found its expression in the formulation of the Rights of Man. Some of these have as their object what are usually called 'the freedoms,' that is to say, ways of recognizing every human being's character as a person responsible for himself and his transcendent destiny, as well as the inviolability of his conscience."

— "Instruction on Christian Freedom and Liberation," Congregation for the Doctrine of the Faith, 1986, 32 bonds to be possible, each person must live in the truth. Freedom is not the liberty to do anything whatsoever. It is the freedom to do good, and in this alone happiness is to be found.

As parents, we are responsible for the blossoming of the free personality of our children, and we do this through administering to them in love, truth and justice. We want them to be "God intoxicated," but in a pure and holy way. The best advice Mark and I ever received about parenting came from Father Joseph Kentenich, founder of the Schoenstatt Apostolic Movement. As a young priest, he worked with a bunch of rebellious high school seminarians from 1912 to 1919. The province had built a new seminary building, and when the students moved into it, they were met with a slew of rules and restrictions. They did not take to it kindly; they fought against it every which way. Rather than battle against their willfulness, Father Kentenich channeled it, challenging these teenage boys to become true heroes in the face of adversity by using the unwanted restrictions to become stronger, more resolute men through self-education, self-discipline, and mutual support.

In short, Father Kentenich's formula was "freedom as much as possible, rules only when necessary." He used this formula as motivation for the boys to place themselves under the protection of Mary and educate themselves to become firm, free, priestly personalities. Whenever possible, he offered them autonomy in planning and decision making and promoted self-discipline and spiritual striving to the highest degree. All of this, of course, was led by his own example. Many of them became outstanding wartime heroes, sacrificing their lives on the battlefield for the cause and in the name of our Blessed Mother.

This principle sounds romantic when we're referring to events that took place a century ago. However, it's still valid today and really works when applied with consistency and love. The trick is to find that which motivates our kids and let them run with it. In order to do this, we have to spend time with them, getting to know them and allowing them to get to know us. When we start to understand their hopes and passions, we start to understand who they are as persons and what "makes them tick." It also gives us a pretty good guess as to how much autonomy we can give them and when.

There's an old adage that my mother-in-law often quoted to me when our kids were small: "Little kids, little problems; big kids, big problems." Mark and I wanted to prepare our kids for the big problems they'd encounter as big kids, and so we began urging them to make their own decisions from the earliest possible moment. The importance of the decision increased with age. Some folks (a.k.a., our children) thought we were mean because once our children reached toddlerhood, we made them choose between one or two toys to play with at a time. When they were done with those, they could put them away and choose a few others. Not only did this lessen the clutter in the house, but more importantly it placed the responsibility of choice into their little hands beginning at a young age. When they were old enough to dress themselves, they could choose which clothes to wear. In the teen years, our advice and guidance always began with the question, "What do you think about …?" or "How would you approach this situation?" Slowly but surely we ushered them into adulthood by placing the responsibility for decisions on them.

This can be an absolutely heartbreaking and most difficult thing to do. No matter how hard we try, there will be times when our kids make decisions with which we disagree. Hard as it is, those are the times during which we have to have confidence in the way we've raised them and trust in God's Divine Providence. Whatever is going on is a part of God's plan for that child. We don't know how God in his wisdom is working on the soul of that child. Once we've granted them autonomy, we can't snatch it back when we perceive things are going awry.

This doesn't mean we've had a rule-free household. Rules are necessary. If the child (regardless of age) is in moral or physical danger, we will speak up and take direct action if necessary. However, we have to repeatedly evaluate the rules we've made. Are they for the children's sake, or ours? Is it something that will help the child to become holy, or something that simply bugs us? In order to tell the difference, we have to be starkly honest with ourselves and have a good grip on our own self-discipline and self-education, and that's not always easy. Our job isn't to assure our own comfort and peace of mind; it's to allow our children to grow up in truth, justice, and freedom.

Our mission is to lead — not push — our children to become what God has intended them to be. We show them how to make decisions and form their lives based on natural and supernatural consequences, not with threats and force. It's so important for us to realize that we're here to make sure they become the "who" they were meant to be from all eternity, to become the "who" they are in God's eyes, not ours. We set them out on this journey by giving them the tools they need for holy self-education. All of the things we've previously mentioned come to the fore here: prayer, Scripture study, spiritual reading, conscience, attitude, acceptance, unity, and the symbols of the domestic church.

We want our children to be interiorly free so that they can remain exteriorly free. Educating for freedom means instilling in them confidence in themselves and trust in God necessary to do his will in all things, no matter how seemingly inconsequential or monumentally difficult. St. Paul explains this to both the Ephesians and the Colossians. "Fathers, do not provoke your children to anger, but bring them up in the discipline and instruction of the Lord" (Eph 6:4). And, "Fathers, do not provoke your children, lest they become discouraged" (Col 3:21).

There are times when our children get angry at us, but what St. Paul means is that we must not force them into resentfulness and negativity. If they become resentful toward us, it won't be long before they become resentful toward God. Eventually, they'll cut off communication with us and the heavenly Father. St. Paul is warning us against robbing our children of their God-given freedom; the freedom by which they come to know and love him on their own terms, within their own souls; the freedom by which they become royal, priestly people according to their baptismal calling. We can't always guarantee joyful cooperation; instead we work to guard against the deep-seated resentfulness that comes from feeling trapped and powerless. We have to set limits for our children, but they must have input into those limits so that eventually they'll become self-limiting. We make the final decisions, but we allow them to exercise their freedom to the fullest possible extent.

When our children feel and experience that, deep down, they are royal children of God, they'll develop the confidence and control that they need to remain regal even in the most dire circumstances and to avoid the riffraff of life. We place the scepter in their hands, figuratively speaking, by offering them the autonomy they need to love, think, decide, and act according to God's will for them, and by fostering in them the ability to discover and become the royal person that God desires them to be. That is the most priceless gift we can ever give them.

Strength for Your Spirit

"When have I educated my children well? … I have educated them well if I have succeeded in making my child ready and able to independently and autonomously live his life as a child of God out of love for God."

— *Father Joseph Kentenich, Servant of God and founder of the Schoenstatt Apostolic Movement*

Strength for Your Family

1. What is your concept of freedom?
2. What rules of your home are absolutely necessary? What rules could you let go?
3. How can you help your children learn to balance freedom and responsibility?
4. Have your children made decisions with which you didn't agree? How did you react? If there was a breech caused, what steps could you take to repair it?

Strength for Your Soul

Prayer of St. Patrick

I arise today
Through the strength of heaven;
Light of the sun,
Splendor of fire,
Speed of lightning,
Swiftness of the wind,
Depth of the sea,
Stability of the earth,
Firmness of the rock.

I arise today
Through God's strength to pilot me;
God's might to uphold me,
God's wisdom to guide me,
God's eye to look before me,
God's ear to hear me,
God's word to speak for me,
God's hand to guard me,
God's way to lie before me,
God's shield to protect me,
God's hosts to save me
Afar and anear,
Alone or in a multitude.
Christ shield me today
Against wounding
Christ with me, Christ before me, Christ behind me,
Christ in me, Christ beneath me, Christ above me,
Christ on my right, Christ on my left,
Christ when I lie down, Christ when I sit down,
Christ in the heart of everyone who thinks of me,
Christ in the mouth of everyone who speaks of me,

Christ in the eye that sees me,
Christ in the ear that hears me.

I arise today
Through the mighty strength
Of the Lord of creation.

— St. Patrick

Chapter Twenty-Four

END ZONE

Most American families enjoy football, and Fenelon Clan is no different. Except for me, that is. I've never understood the game, and so have had very little interest in it. One day, I figured I would actually sit down and watch at least a few minutes of the game with the others. As we watched — or rather as they watched and I sat in complete confusion — I heard Luke say "Donald Driver."

"What did you just say?" I interrupted.

"I said that Donald Driver has the record for the most one thousand-yard career seasons," Luke replied.

"You mean, Donald — as in the name?" I just had to clarify.

"Yeah, Donald Driver," Luke repeated.

"Holy mackerel," I said. "Donald Driver is a *person*?"

Now we'd caught Mark's curiosity. "Yes, Marge. What did you think?"

I could feel my face getting red and hot. Each football season I'd hear "driver this, driver that" on the radio or TV, and I simply assumed I knew what the word meant. "Oh, man," I shook my head. "All this time I thought that was a position, not a player!"

Learning about football is a lot like learning about our Catholic faith. If we don't understand it, we'll have very little interest in it. If we want our kids to be interested in Catholicism, we have to make the time to teach them what it's all about, or it will have no real meaning for them. If our kids don't know the difference between a sacrament and a sacramental, a doctrine and a precept, they'll never really feel as though they are part of the Church. They have to know the rules, field of play, and penalties in order to become actively involved in the faith.

The best way to know about football is to actually play the game. It's one thing to be an avid fan following from the stands or our living room couch; it's another thing to be on the field running the plays. With the ball in our hands, we feel more responsible for carrying out the game plan and are more concerned about the consequences of fumbling. When we're actively involved, everything makes so much more sense, and we feel far more committed to the outcome. The best way to know about our Catholic faith is to actually practice it — to play the game, so to speak. If we want our kids to feel more responsible for carrying out the game plan God has in mind for them, then we have to put the "ball" in their hands and encourage them to run with it. They won't care about the consequences of dropping the ball — sin and ignorance — unless we instill in them religious principles and a hunger for the victory of eternity. Additionally, we need to show our kids how to apply the faith to daily life through service to the family, to the Church, and to the world by way of ecclesial participation and lively apostolate.

Football players are part of a greater whole — the team and, extending beyond that, the conference. They either win together, or they lose together. As Catholics, we are the Chosen People of God, part of a greater whole — our parish and, extending beyond that, the Church — and we know that everyone involved is interdependent through the Communion of Saints. We either win together, or we lose together, because we are the Mystical Body of Christ.

THE MYSTICAL BODY OF CHRIST

"In Bethlehem the Christian people was born, Christ's mystical body, in which each member is closely joined to the others in total solidarity. Our Saviour is born for all. We must proclaim this not only in words, but by our entire life, giving the world a witness of united, open communities where fraternity and forgiveness reign, along with acceptance and mutual service, truth, justice and love."

— *Pope Benedict XVI*, Urbi et Orbi *message,*
Christmas 2006

Fans know when a football player's heart isn't really in it. That's true for us, also. If our hearts aren't really into our faith, or if we're not unconditionally committed to God, then it's just not going to happen. Furthermore, unless we have allegiance to the Church and our trust in the heavenly Father, things will start to fall apart. Without these essentials, we'll never reach the end zone, and this end zone is for all eternity.

Strength for Your Spirit

"For I do not seek to understand that I may believe, but I believe in order to understand. For this also I believe — that unless I believe, I should not understand."

— *St. Anselm*

Strength for Your Family

1. How can you hand your children the ball and encourage them to run with it?
2. What means can you use to instill in your family a hunger for victory (heaven)?
3. How can you help your children understand that they are part of a greater whole?
4. What "game plan" can you devise as a family that will facilitate your unconditional commitment to God?

Strength for Your Soul

A Prayer of Total Commitment

Lord Jesus, let me know myself and know Thee,
And desire nothing save only Thee.
Let me hate myself and love Thee.
Let me do everything for the sake of Thee.
Let me humble myself and exalt Thee.
Let me think nothing except Thee.
Let me die to myself and live in Thee.
Let me accept whatever happens as from Thee.
Let me banish self and follow Thee,
and ever desire to follow Thee.
Let me fly from myself and take refuge in Thee,
that I may deserve to be defended by Thee.
Let me fear for myself, let me fear Thee,
and let me be among those who are chosen by Thee.
Let me distrust myself and put my trust in Thee.
Let me be willing to obey for the sake of Thee.
Let me cling to nothing save only to Thee,
and let me be poor because of Thee.

Look upon me, that I may love Thee.
Call me that I may see Thee,
And forever enjoy Thee.
Amen.

— St. Augustine